CARNIVAL CREATIONS

SM

CRUISE CUISINE FROM CARNIVAL CHEFS

WELCOME ABOARD!

Dear Guests,

Welcome to *Carnival Creations*, cruise cuisine from Carnival chefs featuring mouth-watering recipes created for your kitchen. A fascinating book packed full of recipes that will entertain, inform and often surprise.

To many, dining is the highlight of a Carnival "Fun Ship" cruise and, over the years, we've received literally thousands of recipe requests from our guests. So many, in fact, that we've decided to incorporate a selection of the most popular choices into an "easy to understand" cookbook.

This beautifully illustrated cookbook is filled with page after page of delicious recipes for soups, salads, pasta, entrées, desserts–and for the fitness-conscious, Nautica Spa selections–all sure to tantalize your taste buds. Whether you're cooking an intimate meal for two, or hosting an elegant dinner party featuring some of our nouvelle cuisine, you'll find every dish as easy to prepare as it is to enjoy.

We here at Carnival, the world's most popular cruise line, consistently review our menus, introducing new and exciting foods to keep pace with our guests' ever-changing desires.

I hope you have as much "fun" with these recipes as our chefs did creating them.

Bon Appetit!

Cyrus Marfatia

Cyrus Marfatia
Executive Chef
Carnival Cruise Lines

CONTENTS

APPETIZERS
P. 5

DESSERTS
P. 101

SOUPS,
SALADS,
SIDE DISHES
P. 23

SPA
P. 141

ENTRÉES
P. 51

CHEF'S
NOTES
P. 155

Pictured on cover:
Chocolate Piece de Resistance, p. 119

APPETIZERS

Entertain with style
and finesse. This eclectic
collection of appetizers offers a
range of tastes from simple to
elegant — many of which have
been influenced by different
regions around the world.
Expect the unexpected.

Mussels in Half Shell, p. 6

MUSSELS IN HALF SHELL

SERVES 6

C oveted mostly by Europeans, mussels are perhaps the best-kept secret in the shellfish family. This wonderful version is served with a bubbly turmeric cheese sauce.

TURMERIC CHEESE SAUCE

¼ cup	butter
¼ cup	finely chopped onion
¼ tsp.	minced garlic
¼ cup	all-purpose flour
	Large pinch turmeric
1 cup	fish stock*
¼ cup	white wine
¼ cup	half-and-half
5 oz.	cream cheese, softened
18	frozen mussels in half shell, thawed
¼ cup	grated Parmesan cheese
	Picante sauce

I n 2-quart saucepan melt butter over medium-high heat. Stir in onion and garlic; cook until onion is tender. Stir in flour and turmeric; cook 30 seconds, stirring constantly. Add fish stock, wine and half-and-half; stir until thickened. Reduce heat to low; simmer 15 minutes. Whisk in cream cheese. Season to taste with salt and pepper.

Drain mussels well. Loosen meat from shell; replace meat. Spoon sauce over mussels; sprinkle with Parmesan cheese. Place shells on broiler pan. Broil 4 to 6 inches from heat until bubbly and browned. Spoon picante sauce onto individual serving plates. Arrange 3 mussels over sauce; garnish with chopped parsley.

See Chef's Notes

SALMON TORTILLA

SERVES 6

T his certainly is not a traditional tortilla. The salmon and egg "pancake" should be sliced and garnished with sour cream, salmon caviar and chopped chives.

1 Tbsp.	butter
12 oz.	boneless skinless salmon, chopped
8 oz.	smoked salmon tidbits, chopped
2 cups	thinly sliced potatoes, par-boiled
½ tsp.	minced garlic
¼ cup	thinly sliced onion
10	eggs, well beaten
	Sour cream
	Salmon caviar
	Chopped chives

H eat oven to 350 degrees. In large skillet heat butter over medium-high until hot; stir in all ingredients except eggs. Cook over medium heat until vegetables are cooked. Cool slightly. In large bowl combine salmon mixture with eggs; mix gently. Heat oven-proof non-stick frying pan over low heat until hot. Pour in tortilla mixture. Cook until mixture begins to set around edges.

Place frying pan in oven; bake until eggs are set in center. Garnish with sour cream, salmon caviar and chopped fresh chives.

SCAMPI PROVENÇALE

SERVES 6

One can never have too many shrimp recipes. Here is an exquisite cream sauce served over broiled shrimp and accompanied by an herbed bruschetta.

⅓ cup	clarified butter
½ cup	chopped onion
¾ tsp.	minced garlic
¼ cup	white wine
½ tsp.	cornstarch
1 cup	fish stock*
¼ cup	whipping cream
¼ cup	butter, softened
1	medium tomato, peeled, seeded, chopped
1 tsp.	chopped parsley

BRUSCHETTA

¼ cup	olive oil
½ tsp.	dried oregano leaves
½ tsp.	dried thyme leaves
12	(¼ inch) slices French bread
24	uncooked jumbo shrimp, peeled, deveined

*I*n medium saucepan heat clarified butter over medium-high heat until hot. Stir in onion and garlic; cook until onion is tender. Reduce heat to medium; stir in wine. Cook until wine is reduced by half. Dissolve cornstarch in a little fish stock. Stir remaining fish stock into onion mixture; bring to a boil. Stir in cornstarch mixture; cook, stirring constantly, until thickened. Add whipping cream; cook until heated through. Remove from heat; whisk in softened butter, 1 Tbsp. at a time. Stir in tomato and parsley; season to taste with salt and pepper. Keep warm.

In small bowl combine olive oil, oregano and thyme. Brush oil mixture on both sides of bread slices. Place under broiler until lightly browned.

Season shrimp with salt and pepper. Place on broiler pan. Broil 4 to 6 inches from heat for 4 to 5 minutes or until shrimp turn pink, turning once. To serve, place 4 shrimp on individual serving plates; spoon ⅙ sauce over shrimp. Serve with Bruschetta.

*See Chef's Notes

MENU

C'est Magnifique!

A night made for romance. It begins with the chef's artistry and the fruit of the world's most famous vineyards. Tonight, we dine in the tradition of the finest French cuisine, and toast the magic of Paris.

Grilled Radicchio with Goat Cheese and Roasted Shallots

Escargot Bourgignonne

Onion Soup with Cheese Croutons

Chilled Shrimp Bisque

Penne with Vodka, Tomato and Caviar

Coquilles Saint Jacques

Supreme de Poulet Farcie

Grilled Veal Chop with Herbs de Provence Sauce

Crêpes Suzette

Kahlua Cheesecake

ESCARGOT BOURGIGNONNE

SERVES 6

P lump, juicy escargot might be considered a staple of fine dining. This one calls for anise-flavored liqueur which adds a distinctively different flavor.

¾ cup	butter
2 Tbsp.	minced garlic
1 Tbsp.	finely chopped onion
2 Tbsp.	white wine
1 tsp.	Pernod or anise-flavored liqueur
	Pinch grated nutmeg
1	can escargot, well drained
1 Tbsp.	chopped parsley

I n large frying pan melt butter over high heat; stir in garlic and onion. Cook until vegetables are tender but not brown. Stir in wine, liqueur, nutmeg and escargot; season to taste with salt and pepper. Reduce heat to low; simmer 10 to 15 minutes or until flavors are blended. Sprinkle with parsley.

FROG LEGS WITH RICE NOODLES

SERVES 6

*P*resentation counts in this masterfully created recipe. The stir-fried frog legs are to be arranged on top of a nest of green rice noodles.

6 oz.	rice noodles
1 cup	olive oil
2 cups	cilantro
½ cup	mint leaves
⅓ cup	olive oil
18	frog legs
1 tsp.	green peppercorns
3	red chile peppers, sliced lengthwise
3 inches	galangal (Thai gingerroot), julienned
2 tsp.	fish sauce
1 tsp.	sugar
12	large basil leaves, fried in vegetable oil
2	plum tomatoes, peeled, seeded, finely chopped

*P*lace rice noodles in medium bowl; cover with hot water. Soak for 20 to 30 minutes; drain well. Return to bowl; toss with 1 Tbsp. olive oil. In food processor bowl fitted with metal blade puree cilantro and mint. With motor running, gradually add remaining olive oil.

In large frying pan heat ⅓ cup olive oil until hot over high heat. Add frog legs and green peppercorns; stir-fry 2 to 3 minutes. Add chile peppers, galangal, fish sauce and sugar; mix well. Continue cooking 2 minutes longer.

Gradually add cilantro sauce to noodles tossing until noodles turn green. Arrange noodles like a nest on individual serving plates; place 3 frog legs going in 3 different directions over noodles. Garnish with fried basil leaves and chopped tomato.

TEQUILA LIME SHRIMP

SERVES 6

*T*equila, lime and shrimp are as compatible as this recipe and invited guests. It's sure to become a quick appetizer favorite.

1 Tbsp.	vegetable oil
½ tsp.	minced garlic
1¼ lb.	uncooked shrimp, peeled, deveined
1 lb.	fresh linguine
2 Tbsp.	chopped cilantro

BEURRE BLANC

1 cup	white wine
¼ cup	chopped onion
1 tsp.	lime juice
¼ tsp.	chopped fresh thyme
1	bay leaf
1 cup	whipping cream
1 Tbsp.	roux*
6 Tbsp.	butter, softened
¼ cup	tequila

*I*n small bowl combine oil, garlic and salt and pepper to taste. Coat shrimp with oil mixture. Cover; refrigerate 1 hour.

Prepare linguine according to package directions; drain. Toss with cilantro; keep warm.

In small saucepan combine wine, onion, lime juice, thyme and bay leaf. Cook over high heat until mixture is reduced by half and onion is tender. Stir in cream and roux. Reduce heat to medium. Continue cooking, stirring constantly, until thickened. Simmer until cream is reduced by half. Remove bay leaf. Remove from heat. Slowly whisk in butter, a little at a time. Stir in tequila; season to taste with salt and cracked pepper. Keep warm.

Heat large non-stick frying pan over medium-high heat until hot. Add shrimp; cook until shrimp turn pink. Stir shrimp into sauce.

Serve shrimp mixture over linguine.

*See Chef's Notes

French Crêpes

SERVES 6

*F*anciers of mushrooms, especially the wild variety, will really enjoy these hollandaise-topped delights.

MADAGASCAR HOLLANDAISE

2	egg yolks
3 Tbsp.	clarified butter
2 Tbsp.	white wine
1 tsp.	green peppercorns, cracked
¼ tsp.	chopped parsley

½ cup	whipping cream
1 oz.	dried porcini mushrooms
1 Tbsp.	clarified butter
2 Tbsp.	chopped onion
¼ tsp.	minced garlic
¼ cup	white wine
½ cup	sliced mushrooms
½ cup	sliced wild mushrooms
1 cup	chopped smoked turkey breast
1 tsp.	chopped parsley
12	crêpes*

*P*lace egg yolks in top of double boiler; whisk until thickened slightly and pale yellow. Place double boiler over low heat; cook, whisking constantly until yolks have thickened and bottom of pan is visible between strokes. Remove from heat; slowly whisk in clarified butter, drop by drop. Stir in white wine, peppercorns and parsley. Season to taste with salt. Keep warm over warm water.

In small saucepan heat cream over medium heat until reduced by half; set aside. Place porcini mushrooms in small bowl; cover with hot water. Let stand for ½ hour. Drain, saving liquid. Strain liquid through coffee filter to remove all grit. Chop mushrooms. In large frying pan heat 1 Tbsp. clarified butter until hot. Stir in onion and garlic; cook until onion is tender. Stir in wine; cook until wine is reduced by half. Add porcini mushrooms and cook briefly. Add remaining mushrooms; cook until liquid is almost evaporated. Stir in soaking liquid; cook until liquid is reduced by half. Stir in smoked turkey, parsley and reduced cream. Season to taste with salt.

Fold warm crêpes into quarters. Place 2 on oven-proof serving plate; place ⅙ filling on one side. Top with hollandaise. Repeat with remaining mixture. Place plates under broiler until browned and bubbly.

See Chef's Notes

Heat Cured Atlantic Salmon

SERVES 6

A kaleidoscope of colors and flavors are picked up with the thinly sliced smoked salmon. It is indeed a savory choice.

CONDIMENTS

1 Tbsp.	finely chopped green bell pepper
1 Tbsp.	finely chopped red bell pepper
1 Tbsp.	finely chopped red onion
1 Tbsp.	finely chopped cooked egg white
1 Tbsp.	capers
1½ tsp.	snipped fresh chives
1 lb.	peppered smoked salmon
	Fresh chives

*I*n small bowl combine condiments. Sprinkle generously on individual serving plates. Slice smoked salmon very thin. Place over condiments. Garnish with chives arranged in crisscross fashion.

SATAY OF CHICKEN

SERVES 6

*T*hese Indonesian shish kebabs are easy to prepare and always well received. They may be broiled or grilled over charcoal depending upon personal preference.

1 Tbsp.	vegetable oil
1 Tbsp.	soy sauce
1 Tbsp.	peanut butter
½ tsp.	minced garlic
½ tsp.	minced gingerroot
1 lb.	chicken tenderloins
12	green onions, each about 2 inches long

PEANUT SAUCE

2 Tbsp.	vegetable oil
¼ tsp.	Thai red curry paste
3 Tbsp.	peanut butter
1 tsp.	sugar
½ cup	coconut milk
½ cup	chicken stock or broth*
1 Tbsp.	chopped cilantro
½ tsp.	Thai fish sauce
6	basil leaves, chopped

*I*n small bowl combine oil, soy sauce, peanut butter, garlic and gingerroot; whisk until smooth. Spread mixture over chicken. Cover; refrigerate for 4 to 6 hours.

In small saucepan heat oil until hot over medium-high heat; stir in red curry paste. Cook briefly to release flavors. Add peanut butter and sugar; stir until smooth. Add coconut milk; cook until milk is reduced slightly. Stir in chicken stock; cook until stock is reduced slightly. Stir in cilantro, fish sauce and basil. Keep warm.

Thread chicken onto 12 wooden skewers; place green onion on end of each. Place on broiler pan. Broil 4 to 6 inches from heat 4 to 6 minutes or until chicken is no longer pink, turning once.

Spoon about 2 Tbsp. peanut sauce into center on individual serving plate. Place cooked skewers crisscross over sauce. Sprinkle with chopped green onions.

*See Chef's Notes

Tip: Chicken skewers can be grilled over medium-hot coals until chicken is no longer pink in center.

FRIED OYSTERS, REMOULADE

SERVES 6

*F*orego Oysters on the Half Shell this one time to try this tempting taste alternative. The oysters are deep-fried and then served with a lively dipping sauce.

REMOULADE

1 cup	mayonnaise
2 Tbsp.	chopped onion
2 Tbsp.	chopped dill pickle
2 Tbsp.	chopped capers
1 Tbsp.	chopped fresh dill
1 Tbsp.	chopped red bell pepper
1½ tsp.	lemon juice
1 tsp.	chopped parsley
½ tsp.	minced garlic
1	chopped hard-cooked egg
1 lb.	shucked oysters
1	egg, well beaten
½ cup	seasoned bread crumbs
	Vegetable oil for frying

*I*n medium bowl combine all ingredients for Remoulade; season to taste with salt and white pepper. Chill.

Drain oysters; pat dry. Place egg in shallow dish. Dip oysters in egg; coat with crumbs. Heat oil to 375 degrees. Deep fry oysters until golden brown; drain. Serve with Remoulade.

GRILLED RADICCHIO WITH GOAT CHEESE AND ROASTED SHALLOTS

SERVES 6

*T*his salad-like appetizer is truly out of the ordinary. The radicchio is grilled along with the goat cheese and served with another favorite vegetable, Belgian endive.

MARINADE

2 Tbsp.	olive oil
1 Tbsp.	chopped onion
1 Tbsp.	balsamic vinegar
¼ tsp.	chopped fresh thyme
¼ tsp.	minced garlic
	Cracked black pepper
1	large head radicchio
2 Tbsp.	olive oil
18	peeled whole shallots
¼ tsp.	minced garlic
8 oz.	goat cheese
½ cup	fresh bread crumbs
¼ tsp.	minced garlic
	Pinch chopped fresh thyme
	Pinch chopped fresh oregano
	Cracked black pepper
18 leaves	Belgian endive

*I*n small jar with tight-fitting lid combine ingredients for marinade; season to taste with salt and cracked pepper. Shake well. Cut radicchio into 2 halves leaving stem attached. Cut each half into 6 wedges. (It is important that the leaves remain attached to the stem.) Place in shallow dish; cover with marinade. Marinate 1 hour before serving.

In medium frying pan heat olive oil over medium-high heat until hot. Add shallots and garlic; cook until tender.

Shape goat cheese into 6 rounds. In small bowl combine bread crumbs, garlic, herbs and pepper. Coat goat cheese rounds well with crumb mixture.

Place radicchio wedges on broiler pan. Broil 4 to 6 inches from heat 3 to 5 minutes or until lightly browned. Place cheese rounds and shallots on broiler pan. Broil 4 to 6 inches from heat for 3 to 5 minutes or until cheese is golden.

Arrange 3 Belgian endive leaves toward top of each salad plate. Place 2 wedges of radicchio on top of endive with stems resting on the base of the endive. Place cheese round and 3 shallots at base of radicchio.

PIZZA JARDINIERE

SERVES 6

*I*ndividual pizzas make a fashionable appetizer. This one is filled with fresh ingredients guaranteed to please the palate.

¼ cup	garlic cloves, peeled
¼ cup	olive oil
½ tsp.	cracked black pepper
6	individual pizza shells
2 Tbsp.	sliced green bell pepper
2 Tbsp.	sliced red bell pepper
2 Tbsp.	sliced onion
2 Tbsp.	sliced mushrooms
2 Tbsp.	sliced sun-dried tomatoes
2 Tbsp.	chopped fresh cilantro
2 Tbsp.	chopped fresh basil
1 Tbsp.	chopped fresh oregano
¼ cup	crumbled goat cheese
¼ cup	crumbled blue cheese
¼ cup	crumbled feta cheese
¼ cup	shredded mozzarella cheese

*H*eat oven to 400 degrees. Rub garlic with olive oil; sprinkle with pepper. Place in baking pan; roast about 15 to 25 minutes or until golden brown. Blend into paste. Spread garlic paste onto each pizza shell. Divide all remaining ingredients evenly onto pizza shells. Bake 15 to 20 minutes or until crust is golden brown and crusty.

SAUTÉED MUSHROOMS, CHAMPAGNE SAUCE

SERVES 6

*C*elebrate the deliciousness of mushrooms drenched in creamy champagne sauce.

1 ½ cups	half-and-half
2 Tbsp.	roux*
2	bay leaves
1 Tbsp.	butter
2 Tbsp.	finely chopped onion
½ cup	champagne
½ tsp.	chicken base
½ cup	whipping cream
1 Tbsp.	butter
1 lb.	cremini mushrooms, quartered
1 Tbsp.	chopped parsley
1 ½ tsp.	chopped fresh tarragon
1 ½ tsp.	chopped fresh thyme

*I*n small saucepan heat half-and-half, roux and bay leaves over medium-high heat, stirring constantly, until mixture comes to a boil. Keep warm. In medium saucepan melt butter over medium-high heat until hot. Stir in onion; cook until onion is tender. Stir in champagne and half-and-half mixture. Reduce heat to low; simmer 20 minutes. Stir in chicken base and cream. Strain; keep warm.

In large frying pan melt butter over medium-high heat until hot. Add mushrooms; cook until tender, stirring often. Stir mushrooms into warm sauce; add chopped parsley, tarragon and thyme. Season to taste with salt and pepper.

*See Chef's Notes

Tip: Steam mushrooms for 1½ minutes before sautéing to preserve white color.

SMOKED SALMON PARCELS

SERVES 6

*G*ood things do come in small packages. Here you fold a tasty crab mixture inside smoked salmon slices and place them on assorted greens with caviar and chives.

VINAIGRETTE

1 cup	olive oil
½ cup	white wine vinegar
1½ tsp.	Dijon mustard
	Pinch sugar
6 oz.	crabmeat
½ cup	chopped, seeded, peeled cucumber
⅓ cup	diced avocado
⅓ cup	chopped, seeded, peeled Roma tomato
12	(1 oz. each) slices smoked salmon
2 oz.	caviar
6 cups	assorted salad greens
6	chive tops

*I*n small jar with tight-fitting lid combine olive oil, vinegar, mustard, sugar and salt and pepper to taste; shake well. In medium bowl mix crabmeat, cucumber, avocado and tomato with 3 Tbsp. vinaigrette. Divide crab mixture onto smoked salmon slices. Fold each into a neat parcel. Toss salad greens with 3 Tbsp. vinaigrette; place on individual salad plates. Place parcels over greens. Garnish with chive tops; drizzle additional dressing on plate, if desired.

FRIED CALAMARI WITH SALSA PICANTE

SERVES 6

*O*ften the preferred way to enjoy squid, fried calamari is a popular hors d'oeuvre. Note the clever way to serve the picante dipping sauce.

1½ lb.	cleaned squid rings
	Milk
1 cup	all-purpose flour
1 Tbsp.	paprika
	Shortening for frying
1½	red onions
1 cup	picante sauce

*P*lace squid in large bowl; cover with milk. Refrigerate 1 hour. Mix flour, paprika and salt and white pepper to taste. Remove rings from milk; coat with flour mixture. Heat shortening to 375 degrees. Fry squid until golden brown; keep warm. Cut red onions into quarters; spoon picante sauce into each quarter. Place on serving plates. Serve about 4 oz. fried squid around each sauce-filled onion.

SOUPS, SALADS, SIDE DISHES

This is a unique selection of

the most popular, most often

requested side dishes. There are

hot and cold weather soups,

savory salads and sumptuous

side dishes. Some are simple.

Others are more daring.

All are delightfully delicious.

Fresh Garden Salad in a Walnut
Vinaigrette with Sliced Pears, p. 24

FRESH GARDEN SALAD IN A WALNUT VINAIGRETTE WITH SLICED PEARS

SERVES 6

*T*his crunchy, sweet salad offers an extraordinarily unique taste sensation.

2 firm ripe pears

VINAIGRETTE

¼ cup chopped onion
3 Tbsp. chopped walnuts
½ cup walnut oil
3 Tbsp. pear vinegar

6 to 9 cups garden salad greens

*P*eel and core pears. Poach in light syrup until tender. Slice when cool enough to handle. Chill slices in syrup.

In small jar with tight-fitting lid combine vinaigrette ingredients; shake well. Season to taste with salt and pepper.

Toss salad greens with vinaigrette. Arrange on individual salad plates. Place 2 to 3 pear slices on each salad.

ZUCCHINI, YELLOW SQUASH AND CARROTS VINAIGRETTE

SERVES 6

*T*his lively salad has the appearance of confetti with a very pleasing zest.

VINAIGRETTE

½ cup olive oil
3 Tbsp. lemon juice
2 Tbsp. chopped parsley
1 tsp. chopped fresh oregano
1 tsp. chopped fresh thyme

1 cup grated carrots
1 cup grated peeled zucchini
1 cup grated peeled yellow squash

12 leaves Belgian endive

*I*n small jar with tight-fitting lid combine dressing ingredients; shake well. In medium bowl combine carrots, zucchini and yellow squash; toss with dressing. Cover; refrigerate at least 1 hour. Season to taste with salt and pepper. Serve marinated vegetables on endive leaves.

TOMATO SLICES AND MOZZARELLA CHEESE

SERVES 6

*C*hoose vine-ripened, summer tomatoes for a sweet juicy flavor that compares with no other.

¼ cup	olive oil
½ cup	fresh basil leaves
1 lb.	fresh mozzarella cheese, sliced
18	slices ripe tomato
6	basil leaves

*I*n blender container combine olive oil and basil leaves. Blend using an on and off method. (Do not allow blender to run long or the basil will turn black.) On individual serving plates spoon scant tablespoon olive oil mixture. Alternate slices of cheese and tomato over dressing. Garnish each serving with basil leaf. Using a pepper mill top each with a few grinds of black pepper.

Tip: Fresh mozzarella cheese is available at many supermarkets and specialty markets.

PENNE SICILIANA

SERVES 6

A meatless pasta side dish that's a complement to the entire menu. Thank goodness for Italian cooks.

1 lb.	uncooked penne pasta
2 cups	basic tomato sauce*
½ cup	whipping cream
1 Tbsp.	olive oil
½ tsp.	minced garlic
2 cups	diced zucchini
1 cup	diced eggplant
¾ cup	cubed mozzarella cheese
¼ cup	grated Parmesan cheese

*C*ook pasta according to package directions; drain. Keep warm. In small saucepan over medium-high heat cook tomato sauce and cream until reduced by half. Meanwhile, in large frying pan heat olive oil until hot over medium-high heat. Add garlic; cook until garlic is tender. Stir in zucchini and eggplant; cook until crisp-tender. Stir in pasta; toss gently. Stir in tomato and cream mixture. Just before serving stir in mozzarella and Parmesan cheese. Season to taste with salt and pepper.

*See Chef's Notes

BEEF BARLEY SOUP

SERVES 6

There are a few soups so chock full of satisfying ingredients that they can be served as a meal. This is one fine example.

2 Tbsp.	margarine
½ lb.	stewing beef, cut into ½-inch chunks
½ cup	chopped onion
1 tsp.	minced garlic
½ cup	chopped carrot
½ cup	diced turnip
½ cup	diced potato
½ cup	chopped tomato
½ cup	sliced mushrooms
½ cup	chopped cabbage
1 Tbsp.	beef base
6 cups	beef stock*
½ cup	medium pearl barley

In 5-quart Dutch oven melt margarine over high heat. Stir in beef, onion and garlic. Cook until onion is tender. Stir in remaining ingredients except barley. Season to taste with salt and pepper. Reduce heat to low; simmer 45 minutes. Meanwhile, place barley in medium saucepan with 2 cups water. Bring to a boil over high heat; cover. Reduce heat to medium; simmer 30 minutes. Add barley to soup; continue cooking until beef and barley are tender.

See Chef's Notes

ONION SOUP WITH CHEESE CROUTONS

SERVES 6

The aroma of this great soup as it's cooking is just as remarkable as the taste.

2 Tbsp.	margarine
3 cups	sliced onions
¼ tsp.	minced garlic
8 cups	beef stock*
1 tsp.	chopped fresh thyme
½ tsp.	beef base
2	bay leaves
¼ cup	white wine

CHEESE CROUTONS

6	(½ inch) slices French bread
1 Tbsp.	margarine, melted
3 Tbsp.	grated Parmesan cheese
3 Tbsp.	shredded Swiss cheese

In 3-quart saucepan melt margarine over medium-high heat; stir in onions and garlic. Cook, stirring often, until onions become golden brown (about 45 minutes). Stir in beef stock, thyme, beef base and bay leaves. Bring to a boil; reduce heat to low. Simmer 30 minutes or until flavors are blended. Remove bay leaves. Stir wine into soup just before serving. Season to taste with salt and cracked pepper.

Heat oven to 400 degrees. Brush both sides of bread with melted margarine. Sprinkle tops with Parmesan and Swiss cheese. Bake until toasted and cheese is melted.

Spoon soup into serving bowls; top with croutons.

See Chef's Notes

MINESTRONE SOUP WITH PESTO

SERVES 10

This minestrone goes above and beyond in terms of flavor and breadth of ingredients. The pesto is an added bonus.

PESTO

2 cups	fresh basil leaves
¼ cup	chopped walnuts
¼ cup	grated Parmesan cheese
1 tsp.	minced garlic
1 cup	olive oil

2 Tbsp.	margarine
¼ cup	chopped bacon
½ cup	chopped carrot
½ cup	chopped onion
½ cup	chopped leek
½ cup	chopped cabbage
½ cup	sliced green beans
½ cup	sliced mushrooms
½ cup	chopped tomato
½ cup	chopped spinach leaves
½ cup	cooked white beans
¼ cup	chopped celery
¼ cup	corn
8 cups	beef stock*
2 lb.	ham bone
3 Tbsp.	tomato paste
1 tsp.	minced garlic
1 tsp.	chopped fresh basil
1 tsp.	chopped fresh oregano
3	bay leaves
½ cup	diced potato
2 Tbsp.	chopped parsley
½ cup	cooked elbow macaroni
	Parmesan cheese

Place all pesto ingredients except oil in blender container; blend on high speed until a puree is formed. With blender running, add oil; blend until paste is formed.

In 5-quart Dutch oven melt margarine over medium-high heat. Add bacon; cook until crisp. Add carrot, onion, leek, cabbage, green beans, mushrooms, tomato, spinach, white beans, celery and corn. Cook, stirring occasionally, 10 minutes. Stir in stock, ham bone, tomato paste, garlic, basil, oregano and bay leaves. Bring to a boil. Reduce heat to low; simmer 30 minutes. Add potato; simmer 15 minutes. Add parsley; season to taste with salt and pepper. Remove ham bone and bay leaves. Stir in half of pesto and cooked macaroni. Serve soup with Parmesan cheese and remaining pesto.

MENU

CAPTAIN'S GALA DINNER

The master summons all who sail with him to dine as royal guests in a spectacular celebration of the seagoing life. All aboard are to heed the Captain's wishes of making merry on this special occasion. The Captain has ordered the very best of everything for his guests. On his night, he salutes each of you.

❧

TOMATO SLICES AND MOZZARELLA CHEESE
HEAT CURED ATLANTIC SALMON
FROG LEGS WITH RICE NOODLES

❧

CREAM OF BROCCOLI SOUP
CHILLED STRAWBERRY SOUP

❧

CAESAR SALAD

❧

PENNE SICILIANA
GRILLED JUMBO SHRIMP SERVED OVER MUSHROOM RISOTTO
OAK-SMOKED PORK LOIN WITH CHAMPAGNE CABBAGE
TOURNEDOS OF BEEF TENDERLOIN

❧

CHOCOLATE PIECE DE RESISTANCE

CAESAR SALAD

SERVES 6

*T*here certainly is no other salad more popular than this. Everyone claims to have the best recipe. This one is extremely easy and especially nice. Be sure to use only fresh grated Parmesan.

DRESSING

2	egg yolks
1 Tbsp.	lemon juice
1 Tbsp.	white vinegar
1 tsp.	chopped anchovy fillet
1 tsp.	Worcestershire sauce
½ tsp.	minced garlic
1 cup	vegetable oil
1	head romaine lettuce, torn into bite-size pieces
½ cup	grated Parmesan cheese
1 cup	croutons
	Anchovy fillets, for garnish

*I*n blender container combine all dressing ingredients except oil. Blend on high speed 1 minute. With blender running, slowly add oil; blend until thickened. Chill dressing until ready to serve. In salad bowl toss romaine and Parmesan cheese with ½ cup dressing. Add croutons; toss gently. Garnish with anchovy fillets, if desired.

Tip: Because of food safety, only pasteurized eggs should be used in recipes where the eggs are not cooked.

ÉTOUFFÉE OF LANGOUSTINE WITH GOAT CHEESE ZUCCHINI ROSTI

SERVES 6

A Creole dish of small zucchini cakes topped with creamed goat cheese and vegetables with prawn tails.

ZUCCHINI ROSTI

2	medium zucchini
¼ cup	all-purpose flour
2	eggs, separated
½ tsp.	chopped fresh thyme
½ tsp.	dried oregano leaves
½ tsp.	white pepper
⅛ tsp.	baking powder
½ cup	creamed goat cheese

1½ cups	lobster or shrimp stock
1 Tbsp.	shrimp base
1½ tsp.	paprika
1½ tsp.	gumbo file
½ tsp.	onion powder
½ tsp.	lemon pepper
¼ tsp.	garlic powder
¼ tsp.	dried thyme leaves
¼ tsp.	dried oregano leaves
⅛ tsp.	cayenne pepper
2 Tbsp.	brown roux*
¼ cup	chopped red bell pepper
¼ cup	chopped green bell pepper
¼ cup	chopped yellow bell pepper
¼ cup	chopped onion
1 lb.	frozen cooked langoustine (prawn) tails, thawed

Grate zucchini; salt well. Let stand for 1 hour. Pour off liquid; squeeze dry. Stir in flour, egg yolks, thyme, oregano, pepper and baking powder. In medium bowl beat egg whites until soft peaks form; fold into zucchini mixture. Heat oiled frying pan until hot. Drop spoonfuls of zucchini mixture into hot pan. Cook until golden brown on both sides, turning once. (When cooked cakes should be about 2½-inches diameter and ½-inch thick.) Spoon small amount creamed goat cheese onto each round.

In 3-quart saucepan bring stock to a boil over high heat; add spices. Add roux, stirring constantly, until thickened. Reduce heat to low; simmer 10 minutes. Add vegetables and langoustine. Cook until mixture is heated through.

Serve Étouffée of Langoustine with Rosti.

See Chef's Notes

GAZPACHO ANDALUZ

SERVES 6

A healthy combination of fresh, luscious vegetables creates this exhilarating taste. Chilled soup cups are the ultimate serving vessels.

1½ cups	chopped tomatoes
1 cup	chopped green bell pepper
1 cup	fresh bread crumbs, crust removed
¾ cup	chopped onion
¾ cup	chopped cucumber
¼ cup	chopped green onion
½ tsp.	minced garlic
2 Tbsp.	white vinegar
2 Tbsp.	olive oil
1 Tbsp.	lemon juice
¼ tsp.	dried thyme leaves
¼ tsp.	dried tarragon leaves
¼ tsp.	hot pepper sauce
¼ tsp.	Worcestershire sauce
3 cups	tomato juice

P lace all ingredients except tomato juice in blender container. Blend on high speed until vegetables are finely chopped. Add tomato juice; blend only until well mixed. Season to taste with salt and pepper. Cover; refrigerate overnight. Serve in chilled soup cups. Garnish with diced tomato, cucumbers, green peppers and green onion.

CHILLED CUCUMBER SOUP

SERVES 6

A refreshing idea for a hot summer day. Be sure to add the finishing touch — a garnish of fresh chopped dill.

¼ cup	butter
½ cup	chopped onion
2	bay leaves
2 lb.	diced, seeded, peeled cucumber
2 cups	chicken stock*
1 cup	milk
1 cup	whipping cream
2 Tbsp.	chopped fresh dill

I n 3-quart saucepan melt butter over medium-high heat; add onion and bay leaves. Cook until onion is tender. Stir in cucumber; cook 5 to 10 minutes or until cucumber is tender. Reduce heat to medium. Stir in chicken stock and milk; simmer 5 to 10 minutes or until liquid is reduced. Remove from heat; cool. Remove bay leaves; puree in blender or food processor. Stir in cream; season to taste with salt and white pepper.

Cover; refrigerate overnight. Serve chilled in soup cups; garnish with fresh dill.

*See Chef's Notes

LENTIL SOUP

SERVES 6

A good lentil soup warms the spirit and soothes the soul. This one is no exception.

1 cup	dried lentils
7 cups	beef stock*
¼ lb.	bacon, diced
1 Tbsp.	margarine
¼ cup	chopped onion
¼ cup	chopped carrot
¼ cup	chopped celery
2 Tbsp.	balsamic vinegar
½ tsp.	beef base
¼ tsp.	dried thyme leaves
3	bay leaves

P lace lentils in 5-quart Dutch oven; cover with cold water. Soak overnight; drain. Stir in beef stock. Cook over medium heat 20 to 25 minutes or until tender. In medium frying pan cook bacon over medium-high heat until crisp; remove. Melt margarine. Stir in onion, carrot and celery; cook until vegetables are tender. Stir into lentils. Add bacon, vinegar, beef base, thyme and bay leaves. Reduce heat to low; simmer 30 minutes. Season to taste with salt and pepper; remove bay leaves.

See Chef's Notes

NAVY BEAN SOUP

SERVES 8

C onnoisseurs of bean soup will cherish this recipe. It is extremely full-flavored with all of the smoky goodness ham hocks and bacon provide.

1 lb.	dried navy beans
¼ cup	chopped bacon
½ cup	chopped onion
½ cup	chopped carrot
½ cup	chopped celery
½ tsp.	minced garlic
8 cups	stock or water
1 lb.	ham hocks
¼ tsp.	dried oregano leaves
¼ tsp.	paprika
2	bay leaves
1 Tbsp.	chopped parsley

P lace beans in 5-quart Dutch oven; cover with cold water. Soak overnight; drain. In large frying pan cook bacon over medium-high heat until crisp; remove bacon. Stir in onion, carrot, celery and garlic; cook 5 minutes. Stir onion mixture into beans. Add stock, ham hocks, bacon, oregano, paprika and bay leaves. Bring mixture to a boil over medium-high heat. Reduce heat to medium; simmer beans 1 hour 15 minutes or until tender. Season to taste with salt and pepper. Remove ham hocks and bay leaves. Sprinkle with chopped parsley.

CHICKEN SALAD ON FRENCH BAGUETTE

SERVES 6

N ow there's no question as to what to serve with chicken salad. The pasta salad makes a complete meal.

8 oz.	uncooked rotini pasta
1 cup	broccoli florets
½ cup	chopped carrot
¼ cup	chopped onion
¼ cup	chopped red bell pepper
¼ cup	chopped green bell pepper
5 tsp.	vegetable oil
2 tsp.	white vinegar
1 tsp.	salt
½ tsp.	white pepper
	Pinch dried oregano leaves
3 cups	chopped cooked chicken
½ cup	chopped celery
½ cup	chopped onion
1 cup	mayonnaise
2	loaves French bread
3 cups	shredded iceberg lettuce
6	slices tomato
6	Bibb lettuce leaves

C ook pasta according to package directions; drain. Rinse with cold water. In large bowl combine pasta, broccoli, carrot, onion and red and green peppers; toss. In small jar with tight-fitting lid combine oil, vinegar, salt, pepper and oregano; shake well. Toss pasta mixture with dressing. Refrigerate at least 2 hours before serving.

In medium bowl combine chicken, celery, onion and mayonnaise. Season to taste with salt and white pepper. Chill until serving time.

Slice bread lengthwise in half. Arrange shredded lettuce on bottoms. Top with chicken salad, tomato slices and tops of bread. Cut each baguette on diagonal into sandwiches about 4 inches long.

Place Bibb lettuce leaf on individual plate; spoon rotini salad onto lettuce. Serve with chicken salad sandwich.

Tip: Broccoli and carrots can be steamed briefly, if desired, before mixing with rotini

CHILLED STRAWBERRY

SERVES 6

A sweet, creamy soup that's delightfully decadent.

2 cups	frozen strawberries
2 cups	milk
1 cup	whipping cream
½ cup	sour cream
	Sugar

P lace all ingredients in blender container. Blend on high until smooth. Add sugar to taste. Chill overnight. Serve in chilled soup cups.

Black Bean Soup

SERVES 6

Protein-rich black beans are another food that's gaining in popularity. This is an exceptional way to enjoy them.

1 lb.	dried black beans
12 cups	beef stock*
¼ cup	olive oil
½ cup	chopped onion
½ cup	chopped carrot
½ cup	chopped celery
2 tsp.	minced garlic
2 Tbsp.	beef base
1 Tbsp.	cumin
1 tsp.	sugar
1 tsp.	chili powder
1 tsp.	chopped fresh oregano
2	bay leaves
1 Tbsp.	chopped parsley
	Chopped red onion
	Sour cream

*P*lace beans in 5-quart Dutch oven; cover with cold water. Soak overnight. Drain; stir in beef stock. Bring mixture to a boil over medium-high heat. Reduce heat to medium; simmer beans 45 to 60 minutes or until tender.

In medium frying pan heat oil until hot over medium-high heat. Stir in onion, carrot, celery and garlic; cook until onion is tender. Add to cooked beans along with beef base, cumin, sugar, chili powder, oregano and bay leaves. Reduce heat to low; simmer 30 minutes. Stir in chopped parsley. Season to taste with salt and pepper; remove bay leaves. Garnish each serving with chopped red onion and sour cream.

*See Chef's Notes

Red Bean Soup

SERVES 6

A hearty red bean and vegetable soup that is abounding with flavor.

1 lb.	dried red beans
6 cups	beef stock*
1 lb.	ham hocks
1 Tbsp.	margarine
¼ cup	chopped onion
¼ cup	chopped celery
1 cup	chopped tomatoes
½ cup	diced potato
½ tsp.	chopped fresh thyme
1	bay leaf
1 Tbsp.	chopped parsley

*P*lace beans in 5-quart Dutch oven; cover with cold water. Soak overnight; drain. Stir in beef stock and ham hocks. Bring mixture to a boil over medium-high heat. Reduce heat to medium; simmer beans 1 hour or until tender.

In small frying pan melt margarine over medium-high heat. Stir in onion and celery; cook until onion is tender. When beans are tender add onion mixture and tomatoes, potato, thyme and bay leaf. Bring to a boil; reduce heat to low. Simmer 30 minutes or until vegetables are tender and flavors are blended. Season to taste with salt and pepper. Remove ham hocks and bay leaf. Sprinkle with chopped parsley.

*See Chef's Notes

CHILLED SHRIMP BISQUE

SERVES 6

An exquisite prelude to the feature presentation. Expect nothing short of magnificent.

1 Tbsp.	margarine
¼ cup	finely chopped onion
¼ cup	finely chopped celery
1 tsp.	shrimp base
½ tsp.	paprika
2 cups	fish stock*
½ cup	milk
1 tsp.	salt
1	bay leaf
	Hot pepper sauce
½ cup	half-and-half
1 Tbsp.	cornstarch
1 cup	coarsely chopped baby shrimp
¼ cup	dry sherry
1½ tsp.	lemon juice

In 3-quart saucepan melt margarine over medium-high heat. Stir in onion and celery; cook until onion is tender. Stir in shrimp base and paprika; cook 5 minutes. Add fish stock, milk, salt, bay leaf and a few drops hot pepper sauce. Reduce heat to low; simmer 15 minutes. Add half-and-half; bring soup back to a boil. Dissolve cornstarch in 1 Tbsp. water or fish stock; stir into soup. Cook, stirring constantly, until thickened. Stir in shrimp, sherry and lemon juice. Remove from heat.

Cover; refrigerate overnight. Serve soup chilled.

See Chef's Notes

BOUILLABAISSE

SERVES 6

This famous fish chowder includes such a wonderful variety of succulent seafood, one taste and you can almost feel the salt in the air.

2 Tbsp.	olive oil
¼ cup	chopped onion
¼ cup	chopped leek
¼ cup	chopped fresh fennel
¼ cup	chopped celery
1 tsp.	minced garlic
2	bay leaves
3 cups	seafood stock
½ cup	diced tomato
½ cup	white wine
	Juice from ½ orange
¼ tsp.	chopped fresh thyme
	Small pinch saffron
8 oz.	fresh fish fillets, diced
6 oz.	uncooked shrimp, peeled, deveined
4 oz.	mussels, scrubbed
4 oz.	scallops
4 oz.	lobster meat, if desired
4 oz.	chopped clams

In 5-quart Dutch oven heat 1 Tbsp. oil until hot over medium-high heat; stir in onion, leek, fennel, celery, garlic and bay leaves. Cook until onion is tender. Stir in seafood stock, tomato, wine, orange juice, thyme and saffron. Cover; bring to a boil. Reduce heat to low; simmer 10 minutes.

In large frying pan heat remaining 1 Tbsp. oil over medium-high heat until hot. Add fish, shrimp, mussels, scallops and lobster; cook until shrimp turn pink. Add to stock mixture; simmer 3 to 4 minutes. Add clams; continue cooking until all seafood is cooked. Remove bay leaves; season to taste with salt and pepper.

CHICKEN AND OKRA SOUP

SERVES 6

A spicy New Orleans recipe filled with delicious vegetables, chicken and rice.

6 Tbsp.	margarine
½ tsp.	minced garlic
½ cup	chopped onion
½ cup	chopped carrot
½ cup	chopped celery
½ cup	chopped red bell pepper
½ cup	chopped green bell pepper
6 cups	chicken stock*
2 Tbsp.	Cajun spices*
1 tsp.	chopped fresh thyme
1 tsp.	chopped fresh oregano
½ cup	brown roux*
2 Tbsp.	gumbo file
1 lb.	okra, sliced ½-inch thick
1 Tbsp.	vegetable oil
2 cups	chopped cooked chicken
1½ cups	cooked rice
½ cup	chopped green onions

*I*n 3-quart saucepan melt margarine over medium-high heat. Stir in garlic; cook 1 minute. Stir in onion, carrot, celery and red and green peppers. Cook until onion is tender. Stir in chicken stock, Cajun spices, thyme and oregano; bring to a boil. Reduce heat to medium; stir in roux and gumbo file. Cook, stirring constantly, until soup is thickened. Reduce heat to low; simmer 30 minutes or until flavors are blended. Season to taste with salt and pepper.

Meanwhile, in frying pan cook okra in oil until tender. Stir chicken, rice and okra into soup; cook until heated through. Stir in chopped green onions.

See Chef's Notes

GREEK SALAD

SERVES 6

*T*he perfect blend of vegetables with a simple vinaigrette – wonderful.

VINAIGRETTE

½ cup	olive oil
¼ cup	white vinegar
1 Tbsp.	prepared mustard
3 cups	shredded lettuce
3	medium tomatoes, diced
2	medium cucumbers, diced
½ cup	sliced black olives
½ cup	crumbled feta cheese
1 Tbsp.	chopped parsley

*I*n jar with tight-fitting lid combine olive oil, vinegar and mustard; shake well. Season to taste with salt and pepper.

In large bowl combine lettuce, tomatoes, cucumbers, olives and feta cheese. Add ½ cup vinaigrette; toss gently. Sprinkle with parsley.

CREMA FUNGHI

SERVES 6

A creamy mushroom soup that just can't compare. Even the name has a touch of elegance.

2 Tbsp.	butter
2½ cups	chopped mushrooms
¼ cup	chopped onion
½ tsp.	minced garlic
¼ cup	brandy
3 cups	chicken stock*
1 cup	half-and-half
¼ cup	roux*
1 Tbsp.	porcini powder
2	bay leaves
¼ cup	whipping cream

*I*n large frying pan melt butter over high heat; stir in mushrooms, onion and garlic. Cook, stirring often, until mushrooms are tender. Add brandy; continue cooking, stirring constantly, until reduced by half. Stir in stock, half-and-half, roux, porcini powder and bay leaves. Cook, stirring constantly, until thickened. Reduce heat to low; simmer 5 to 10 minutes. Season to taste with salt and pepper; remove bay leaves. Stir in whipping cream.

*See Chef's Notes

ORIENTAL PEKADILYO SOUP

SERVES 6

*T*his is a soup that nourishes like a stew. It's filled with all of the finer ingredients in life.

½ lb.	coarsely ground beef
½ lb.	coarsely ground pork
½ cup	finely chopped leek
½ cup	finely chopped potato
½ cup	finely chopped tomato
½ cup	finely chopped cabbage
¼ cup	finely chopped red bell pepper
¼ cup	finely chopped green bell pepper
½ tsp.	minced garlic
8 cups	beef stock*
2 Tbsp.	tomato paste
1 tsp.	beef base
1 tsp.	soy sauce
2	bay leaves

*I*n 5-quart Dutch oven cook beef, pork, leek, potato, tomato, cabbage, red and green peppers and garlic over medium-high heat until lightly browned. Stir often so mixture does not burn. Stir in remaining ingredients. Reduce heat to low; simmer 1 hour. Remove bay leaves.

*See Chef's Notes

GREEN SPLIT PEA SOUP WITH SMOKED SAUSAGE

SERVES 6

*A*t first glance, this pea soup resembles most other recipes with the exception of smoked sausage and mint leaves. Those two additions make it exceptional indeed.

1 lb.	dried split peas
8 cups	chicken stock*
1 tsp.	chopped fresh thyme
½ tsp.	white pepper
½ tsp.	ham base
6 to 8	fresh mint leaves
2	bay leaves
1 Tbsp.	margarine
8 oz.	diced smoked sausage
½ cup	chopped onion
¼ cup	chopped carrot
¼ cup	chopped celery

*P*lace split peas, chicken stock, thyme, pepper, ham base, mint leaves and bay leaves in 5-quart Dutch oven. Cook over medium heat 45 to 60 minutes or until tender. In medium frying pan melt margarine over medium-high heat. Add sausage; cook several minutes until lightly browned. Stir in onion, carrot and celery; cook until vegetables are tender. Stir into split pea mixture. Continue cooking 10 to 15 minutes or until vegetables are cooked and flavors are blended. Season to taste with salt; remove bay leaves.

See Chef's Notes

SHRIMP SALAD WITH LOW-CAL 1000 ISLAND DRESSING

SERVES 6

*T*his light salad is so loaded with goodness, the calories aren't even missed.

SHRIMP SALAD

1 lb. 4 oz.	cooked baby shrimp
½ cup	diced tomato
¼ cup	chopped onion
¼ cup	chopped celery
1 cup	reduced-calorie 1000 island dressing
2 cups	shredded iceberg lettuce
1 cup	shredded chicory
12	slices tomato
18	slices cucumber
12	pitted black olives
3	hard-cooked eggs, quartered lengthwise

*I*n large bowl combine shrimp, tomato, onion, celery and dressing; mix gently. Season to taste with salt and pepper.

Line 6 individual plates with lettuce and chicory; spoon shrimp salad onto lettuce. Garnish each with 2 tomato slices, 3 cucumber slices, 2 olives and 2 egg quarters.

CREAM OF BROCCOLI SOUP

SERVES 6

*T*his rich, mouth-watering soup can easily be enjoyed as a whole meal. A loaf of warm whole grain bread is a must.

¼ cup margarine
1¼ lb. chopped fresh broccoli
½ cup chopped onion
½ tsp. minced garlic
2 cups chicken stock*
2 cups milk
1 Tbsp. chicken base
2 bay leaves
Pinch grated nutmeg
½ cup roux*
2 cups half-and-half

*I*n 3-quart saucepan melt margarine over medium-high heat. Stir in broccoli, onion and garlic; cook until onion is tender. Stir in stock, milk, chicken base, bay leaves and nutmeg; mix well. Stir in roux; continue cooking, stirring constantly, until soup is thickened. Reduce heat to low; simmer 30 minutes. Stir in half-and-half; season to taste with salt and pepper. Remove bay leaves. Cook over low heat until soup is heated through.

See Chef's Notes

NATIVE BEANS SALAD

SERVES 6

A new and improved version of the "three bean salad." This delightful combination of ingredients will definitely tingle your taste buds.

DRESSING

2 Tbsp. malt vinegar
2 Tbsp. vegetable oil
1 tsp. cumin
½ tsp. Worcestershire sauce
¼ tsp. chopped fresh oregano
¼ tsp. chopped fresh thyme

¾ cup cooked wax beans
¾ cup cooked green beans
¾ cup cooked navy beans
¾ cup cooked black beans
¾ cup cooked red beans
½ cup chopped cilantro

*I*n small jar with tight-fitting lid combine dressing ingredients; shake well. In large bowl mix all salad ingredients together; toss with dressing. Season to taste with salt and pepper. Cover; refrigerate at least 6 hours. Serve salad chilled.

Tip: Canned beans are an acceptable substitute for cooked navy, black and red beans.

SOPA DE CARACOL

SERVES 6

A savory Mexican soup made with plantain, yucca, coconut milk and fresh conch.

2 Tbsp.	margarine
1 lb.	ground conch meat
¼ cup	chopped onion
1 tsp.	minced garlic
½ cup	diced plantain
½ cup	diced fresh yucca
½ cup	diced red bell pepper
3 cups	fish stock*
1 cup	coconut milk
½ cup	diced tomato
1 tsp.	fish bouillon powder
½ cup	whipping cream
¼ cup	chopped cilantro

*I*n large saucepan melt margarine over medium heat; stir in conch, onion and garlic. Cook until onion is tender. Stir in plantain, yucca, red bell pepper and fish stock; bring to a boil. Reduce heat to low; simmer 30 minutes. Stir in coconut milk, tomato, fish bouillon and cream. Season to taste with salt and pepper. Garnish each serving with chopped cilantro.

*See Chef's Notes

CREAM OF ASPARAGUS SOUP

SERVES 6

A quick and easy way to enjoy an incredibly delicious vegetable. It's the creamiest.

4 cups	chicken stock*
1 tsp.	chicken base
¼ cup	roux*
1 lb.	fresh or frozen asparagus cuts
2 cups	milk
½ cup	half-and-half
	Pinch grated nutmeg

*I*n medium saucepan bring chicken stock and chicken base to a boil over medium-high heat; stir in roux. Continue cooking, stirring constantly, until thickened. Reduce heat to low. Add asparagus, milk, half-and-half and nutmeg. Season to taste with salt and white pepper. Simmer 15 minutes or until asparagus is crisp-tender.

*See Chef's Notes

ENTRÉES

The finest, most exotic cuisines are represented in this bountiful section. Never before have so many wonderful flavors come together to deliver a more satisfying dining experience. Each distinctively delicious dish is an absolute treasure.

Cilantro Glazed Florida Snapper with Sesame Stir-Fry, p. 52

Cilantro Glazed Florida Snapper with Sesame Stir-Fry

SERVES 4

The colorful presentation of this fabulous fish and vegetable dish is but a prelude to its exquisite taste.

Cilantro Glaze

½ bunch	cilantro, chopped
1 ½ tsp.	minced garlic
¾ tsp.	cumin
⅛ tsp.	ground cardamom
¼ cup	virgin olive oil
2 Tbsp.	virgin olive oil
4	(6 oz. each) fresh Florida Snapper fillets

Sesame Stir-Fry

1 Tbsp.	sesame oil
8	baby zucchini, cut in half lengthwise
8	baby yellow patty-pan squash
8	baby carrots, peeled, stems left on
4 oz.	snow peas

Guacamole
Chopped parsley

*I*n small bowl mix together all glaze ingredients. Season to taste with salt and pepper.

In medium frying pan heat oil until hot over medium-high heat. Place snapper in pan, skin side down; cook 1 minute. Turn; brush cilantro glaze on top of snapper. Cook 2 minutes; brush glaze on second side. Continue cooking until snapper flakes with a fork. Brush with glaze before removing from pan.

Meanwhile, heat sesame oil over high heat in wok or frying pan. Add vegetables; stir-fry until vegetables are crisp-tender.

Place vegetables in center of serving plates; place fish on vegetables. Garnish with a tablespoon of guacamole and chopped parsley.

Rack of Lamb, Natural

SERVES 6

*M*ost epicures believe lamb and veal to be the two most elegant meats. This natural rack of lamb is a case in point. The au jus makes it complete.

2 Tbsp.	vegetable oil
1 Tbsp.	chopped fresh rosemary
1 Tbsp.	minced garlic
1 tsp.	cracked black peppercorns
2	(2 to 2½ lb. each) racks of lamb, Frenched

Au Jus

⅔ cup	chopped onion
⅔ cup	chopped carrot
⅔ cup	chopped celery
1 tsp.	minced garlic
	Few sprigs fresh mint
1	sprig rosemary
1 cup	water

*I*n small bowl combine oil, rosemary, garlic and peppercorns; rub onto lamb. Refrigerate overnight. Heat oven to 350 degrees. Rub lamb with salt; place in roasting pan. Roast 20 to 30 minutes or until desired doneness. Temperature should reach 150 degrees for medium rare. Carve into chops just before serving.

Remove meat; keep warm. Add onion, carrot, celery, garlic, mint, and rosemary to roasting pan. Cook over medium heat until browned; stir in water. Simmer, stirring to remove browned bits from pan, until juices are reduced; strain. Season to taste with salt and pepper. Serve with roasted lamb chops.

Tip: Au jus may be thickened with cornstarch, if desired.

GRILLED JUMBO SHRIMP SERVED OVER MUSHROOM RISOTTO

SERVES 6

*I*talians love their risotto, and this dish is no exception. Grilled or broiled shrimp with garlic butter is the main attraction.

MUSHROOM RISOTTO

½ cup	butter
½ cup	chopped onion
½ tsp.	minced garlic
1	bay leaf
1 lb.	sliced mushrooms
½ cup	white wine
2 tsp.	porcini mushroom powder
2 cups	uncooked rice
6 cups	chicken stock*
½ cup	grated Parmesan cheese
2 Tbsp.	chopped parsley

½ cup	clarified butter
1 Tbsp.	minced garlic
24	uncooked jumbo shrimp, peeled, tail on, deveined
2 Tbsp.	chopped parsley

*I*n 3-quart saucepan melt butter over medium-high heat. Stir in onion, garlic and bay leaf. Cook until onion is tender; stir in mushrooms. Cook, stirring occasionally, until mushrooms begin to brown. Stir in wine and porcini powder; cook 2 minutes. Stir in rice and chicken stock; bring to a boil. Cover; reduce heat to low. Simmer until rice is cooked and liquid absorbed. Stir in Parmesan cheese and parsley before serving.

In medium saucepan heat butter and garlic over medium-high heat until mixture comes to a boil. Remove from heat; keep warm. Place shrimp on broiler pan. Broil 4 to 6 inches from heat 4 to 5 minutes or until shrimp turn pink. Add shrimp to garlic butter; stir to coat well. Arrange 4 shrimp on each serving plate; sprinkle with parsley. Serve with garlic butter and Mushroom Risotto.

*See Chef's Notes

Tip: Shrimp can be cooked over hot coals on a charcoal grill.

FILLET OF FRESH ALASKAN SALMON

SERVES 6

I ndescribably delicious. This salmon has such an array of tremendous tastes, it leaves one speechless.

SALAD

1	red bell pepper, julienned
1	green bell pepper, julienned
1	yellow bell pepper, julienned
1	small head cabbage, shredded
1	leek, julienned
1	carrot, julienned
3	whole cardamom
3	whole cloves
1 tsp.	cumin seeds
1 cup	chopped fresh mint
1 cup	chopped cilantro
½ cup	chopped fresh basil
6	cloves garlic, minced
12 oz.	cream cheese, softened
¼ cup	plain yogurt
3	egg yolks
1 Tbsp.	lime juice
1 tsp.	fish base
6	(6 oz. each) Alaskan salmon fillets

TOMATO AND COCONUT CHUTNEY

2 Tbsp.	vegetable oil
2 oz.	chopped fresh coconut
6	cloves garlic, minced
2 Tbsp.	cumin seed
1 tsp.	minced gingerroot
14 oz.	cherry tomatoes, halved
4	shallots, chopped
1 cup	chopped cilantro
6	pappadam
6	fleurons
	Coconut slices
	Pineapple leaves

In large bowl stir together salad ingredients; cover with ice water. Refrigerate overnight to crisp and curl. Drain well before serving.

In frying pan toast cardamom, whole cloves and cumin seeds over high heat. Remove from heat; grind to a powder. Blend mint, cilantro, basil and garlic into a paste. Stir in cream cheese, yogurt, egg yolks, lime juice and fish base. Coat salmon with yogurt mixture. Cover; refrigerate 2 to 3 hours.

In medium saucepan heat oil until hot; stir in coconut, garlic, cumin seed and gingerroot. Cook until garlic just begins to brown; stir in cherry tomatoes. Cook 2 to 3 minutes to soften. Stir in shallots and cilantro; mix well. Season to taste with salt and pepper. Set aside.

Heat oven to 350 degrees. Place salmon on oiled baking pan. Bake 20 to 30 minutes or until fish flakes with a fork. Place briefly under broiler to brown lightly, if desired.

Cut pappadam into small rounds. Toast on hot griddle to lightly brown. Place hot pappadam inside a 2-oz. ladle to form cup. Remove when cool and pappadam holds cup shape.

Serve salmon with salad. Place tomato and coconut chutney in pappadam cups. Garnish with fleurons, coconut slices and pineapple leaves, if desired.

Paupiettes of Salmon with Shrimp Mousse and Seaweed

Serves 6

*M*agnificence from the sea. Salmon by itself is quite elegant, but this recipe for Paupiettes takes splendor to a whole new level.

Beurre Blanc

¾ cup	butter, softened
1 oz.	pickled ginger, chopped
¾ cup	white wine
6 Tbsp.	white Cinzano
1¼ cups	fish fumet
¾ cup	whipping cream
2 Tbsp.	lemon juice

Shrimp Mousse

4	egg whites
1½ lb.	uncooked shrimp, peeled, deveined
¾ cup	whipping cream
½ cup	white wine
2	egg yolks
3 tsp.	shrimp base
¼ cup	cooked beet or red pepper puree
¼ cup	cooked spinach puree
1 oz.	saffron, soaked in warm water
1½ lb.	salmon fillet
4 to 6	seaweed sheets, cut in half
1 cup	meat from lobster claw
	Fish fumet
1½ cups	tomato concasse*
	Fleurons
	Kaffir lime leaves, fried
	Sliced gingerroot, fried

*I*n medium saucepan heat 1 Tbsp. butter over medium-high heat until hot. Stir in ginger; cook until ginger just begins to brown. Stir in wine and Cinzano; cook until reduced by two-thirds. Add fish fumet; continue cooking until reduced by half. Stir in cream. Cook 3 minutes, stirring constantly. Remove from heat. Slowly whisk in remaining butter, a little at a time. Add lemon juice; season to taste. Keep warm.

In medium bowl beat egg whites until soft peaks form; set aside. Place shrimp in bowl of food processor fitted with metal blade. Process shrimp until paste is formed. Add cream, wine, egg yolks and shrimp base. Process until well blended. Add egg whites; process briefly to keep mixture light. Divide mixture into thirds. Stir beet puree into one third, spinach puree into second third and saffron into remaining third.

Carefully pound salmon fillets to flatten. On each fillet place half sheet of seaweed. Spread each with 2 Tbsp. spinach mousse. Place half sheet seaweed over spinach puree; spread each with beet mousse. Place half sheet seaweed over beet puree; spread with saffron mousse. Top with lobster meat. Carefully roll each tightly to form roulade. Wrap in aluminum foil; twist ends to seal.

In large saucepan heat fish fumet to a simmer over medium-high heat. Place salmon rolls in liquid; reduce heat to low. Poach until center is 110 degrees. Remove from saucepan; let rest for 10 to 15 minutes. Carefully remove foil; slice each diagonally. Place on serving plates; spoon tomato concasse onto plates. Garnish with fleurons, fried lime leaves and fried sliced gingerroot.

*See Chef's Notes

Quenelles of Fresh Alaskan Salmon

Serves 6

This is a true masterpiece. One might think it is too beautiful to eat, but it is best to indulge. It is unforgettable.

	Julienne strips green, red, yellow bell pepper
6	egg whites
3 lb.	salmon, minced
1¼ cups	whipping cream
2	egg yolks
4 tsp.	fish base
3-4 cups	fish stock*
½ lb.	fresh pasta, preferably tri-colored

Mousse

12	morel mushrooms
2	egg whites
6 oz.	scallops
6 Tbsp.	whipping cream
1	egg yolk
1 tsp.	fish base
1 Tbsp.	beet puree
1 Tbsp.	spinach
	Saffron, soaked in warm water
1¼ cups	fish stock*
¾ cup	champagne
	Chopped fresh dill

Place julienne strips of peppers in medium bowl; cover with cold water. Refrigerate overnight to crisp and curl. Drain well before serving.

In medium bowl beat egg whites until soft peaks form; set aside. Place salmon in food processor bowl fitted with metal blade. Process salmon until a paste forms. Add cream, egg yolks and fish base. Process until well blended. Add egg whites; process briefly to keep mixture light. Shape into quenelles (ovals) using 2 to 3 Tbsp. for each. In large saucepan heat fish stock to a simmer over medium-high heat. Place quenelles in liquid; reduce heat to low. Poach until firm outside and internal temperature reaches 110 degrees.

Prepare pasta according to package directions. Drain; keep warm.

Soak morel mushrooms in warm water to soften. In medium bowl beat egg whites until soft peaks form; set aside. Place scallops in food processor bowl fitted with metal blade. Process scallops until paste is formed. Add cream, egg yolk and fish base. Process until well blended. Add egg whites; process briefly to keep mixture light. Divide mixture into thirds. Stir beet puree into one third, spinach puree into second third and saffron into remaining third. Fill tip of morels with some of each color mousse. Poach filled morels in fish stock. Slice into halves. Arrange on plate with quenelles, tri-color pasta and julienned peppers. Pour champagne over quenelles on each plate. Sprinkle dill around edges.

See Chef's Notes

Tip: Homemade pasta can be used. Divide pasta recipe into thirds. Color one third with pureed beets, second third with pureed spinach and remaining third with saffron (soaked in warm water). Roll pasta into sheets; cut into triangles about 1½-inch on a side.

ESCALOPE DE VEAU CALVADOS

SERVES 6

This exceptional French recipe combines veal, apples and mushrooms with a brandy cream sauce.

1 Tbsp.	butter
2 cups	sliced apples
1 cup	mushrooms, quartered
¼ cup	Calvados or apple brandy
1 cup	demi-glace*
½ cup	whipping cream
¼ cup	all-purpose flour
6	(4½ oz. each) veal scallops
2 Tbsp.	vegetable oil

*I*n large frying pan heat butter over high heat; stir in apples and mushrooms. Cook until apples are tender and mushrooms cooked. Meanwhile, in medium saucepan heat brandy. When brandy is hot, carefully ignite. Stir in demi-glace and cream; bring to a boil. Stir in apple mixture. Keep warm.

Place flour in shallow dish; season to taste with salt and pepper. Coat veal with flour mixture. In large frying pan heat oil over medium-high heat until hot. Add veal; cook 3 to 4 minutes for medium, turning once. Serve veal with sauce.

*See Chef's Notes

OSSO BUCCO

SERVES 6

A classic Italian stew that's not at all like Grandma used to make. Pass it on.

1 cup	all-purpose flour
1 tsp.	paprika
4 lb.	veal shanks, cut into 2 to 3-inch pieces
¼ cup	olive oil
½ cup	chopped carrot
½ cup	chopped onion
½ cup	chopped celery
1 tsp.	minced garlic
1 cup	white wine
2 cups	demi-glace*
2 cups	basic tomato sauce*
½ tsp.	grated orange rind
½ tsp.	grated lemon rind
2	bay leaves

GREMOLATA

2 Tbsp.	grated lemon rind
4 tsp.	chopped parsley
2 tsp.	minced garlic

*H*eat oven to 325 degrees. Mix flour with ½ tsp. paprika and salt and pepper to taste. Coat veal shanks well with flour mixture. In 5-quart Dutch oven heat oil until hot over medium-high heat; add meat. Cook until meat is browned on all sides; remove meat and set aside. Add carrot, onion, celery and garlic and sauté until onion is tender. Stir in wine; cook, stirring occasionally, until wine is reduced to about ½ cup. Stir in all remaining ingredients including veal; season to taste with salt and pepper. Cover; bring to a boil. Place in oven; cook 2½ to 3 hours or until meat is tender. Remove bay leaves.

In small bowl combine ingredients for gremolata. Serve with Osso Bucco.

*See Chef's Notes

DARNE DE SALMON

SERVES 6

This superb salmon is smothered in a scallop mousse and served with a fabulous wine and brandy sauce.

SAUCE NANTUA

6 Tbsp.	butter
1 tsp.	vegetable oil
¾ cup	chopped onion
¾ cup	chopped celery
2	cloves garlic, minced
1 lb.	uncooked crayfish in shell, chopped
½ cup	tomato paste
1 cup	brandy
1 cup	white wine
2 cups	whipping cream

MOUSSE

12 oz.	uncooked scallops
½ cup	white wine
½ cup	whipping cream
1	egg
2	egg yolks
1 tsp.	fish base

6	(¾ inch thick) salmon steaks
6	cooked crayfish
6	sprigs fresh dill

*I*n medium frying pan heat butter and oil over medium-high heat until hot. Stir in onion, celery and garlic; cook until onion is tender. Add chopped crayfish with shells. Continue cooking until crayfish begin to brown. Stir in tomato paste; cook until liquid evaporates. Add brandy; carefully ignite. When flames subside stir in white wine; cook until reduced by half. Stir in whipping cream; cook until reduced by half. Strain sauce through cheesecloth; keep warm.

Place scallops in bowl of food processor fitted with steel blade. Process scallops until a paste is formed. Add remaining mousse ingredients; process until well blended. Place over ice bath.

Heat oven to 350 degrees. Spread ⅙ of mousse over each salmon steak. Place in baking pan; cover. Bake 15 to 20 minutes or until salmon flakes with a fork. Broil 4 to 6 inches from heat to brown lightly. Garnish each with cooked crayfish and sprig of dill. Serve with Sauce Nantua.

SPAGHETTI CARBONARA

SERVES 6

A loaf of crusty bread, a bottle of Italian wine and the richest, most wonderful pasta dish ever imagined.

1½ lb.	uncooked spaghetti
½ lb.	bacon, cut up
¼ cup	chopped onion
½ tsp.	minced garlic
1 cup	half-and-half
½ cup	milk
½ cup	whipping cream
1	egg, slightly beaten
¼ cup	grated Parmesan cheese
2 Tbsp.	chopped parsley

*C*ook spaghetti according to package directions; drain. Keep warm.

In large frying pan cook bacon over high heat until golden. Reduce heat to medium; add onion and garlic. Cook 5 minutes. In medium bowl mix half-and-half, milk, whipping cream and egg until well blended. Toss with spaghetti. Add to bacon mixture. Cook over low heat until thoroughly heated. Season to taste with salt and white pepper. Sprinkle with Parmesan cheese and parsley.

HALIBUT PAUPIETTES WITH LOBSTER STUFFING

SERVES 6

This halibut dish makes no excuses for its grandiosity. Everything about it, from the lobster tail stuffing to the caviar garnish, is truly first-class.

LOBSTER MOUSSE

12 oz.	uncooked lobster meat
2	egg whites, lightly beaten
¾ cup	whipping cream
1	egg yolk

LOBSTER SAUCE

2 Tbsp.	vegetable oil
2 lb.	lobster shells
½ cup	chopped leek
3	plum tomatoes, peeled, seeded, chopped
2 Tbsp.	tomato paste
2	cloves garlic, minced
2 cups	chicken stock*
¾ cup	white wine
6	white peppercorns, crushed
	Few sprigs tarragon
1 lb. 6 oz.	unsalted butter, cut into small pieces
	Cayenne pepper

12	(3 oz. each) quarter fillets halibut
20	spinach leaves, blanched, dried
1½ lb.	lobster tails
2 cups	vegetable stock*
¼ cup	unsalted butter
1 cup	diced carrots
1 cup	diced leeks
1 cup	diced celery
½ cup	dry sherry
3 Tbsp.	brandy
1 oz.	dried morels, soaked in cold water 2 hours
¼ cup	unsalted butter, melted

6	cooked lobster claws
6	fleurons
	Red caviar

Dry lobster; sprinkle with salt. Refrigerate 20 minutes; dry lobster. Mince lobster by hand or in blender. Place fine sieve over small bowl; set bowl over ice. Press lobster through sieve. Over ice fold egg whites into lobster. Over ice slowly add cream, stirring constantly. Add egg yolk; season to taste with salt and pepper. Refrigerate 30 minutes or until mixture becomes firm.

In large saucepan heat oil until hot over medium-high heat; stir in lobster shells. Cook until shells begin to brown. Add remaining ingredients except butter and cayenne pepper; reduce heat to low. Simmer 30 minutes, skimming frequently. Strain through cheesecloth; return to heat. Continue cooking until reduced by four-fifths. Slowly, whisk in butter bit by bit. Season to taste with salt and cayenne pepper.

Dry halibut; score skin side lightly. Carefully pound between 2 sheets of plastic wrap until thin. Season to taste with salt and pepper; spread thin layer of lobster mousse over halibut. Turn halibut over; cover skin side with spinach leaves then layer of mousse.

Cook lobster tails in boiling vegetable stock about 5 minutes. Plunge in cold water to cool. Carefully remove from shell keeping tail meat intact. Cut lengthwise into quarters; lay quarters along center of halibut fillet. Roll up; wrap in plastic wrap. Steam over boiling water 8 minutes.

In medium frying pan melt 2 Tbsp. butter; add carrots, leeks and celery. Cook until tender. Spoon onto individual serving plates. Remove plastic wrap from halibut; cut each paupiette crosswise into 3 slices. Place over vegetables. In small saucepan heat sherry until reduced by half. Stir in 1¼ cups lobster sauce, brandy and 2 Tbsp. butter; pour sauce around paupiettes. Drain rehydrated morels; toss with melted butter. Add to plate. Warm lobster claws in steamer. Garnish plates with lobster claws, fleurons and caviar.

*See Chef's Notes

Grilled Veal Chops with Herbs de Provence Sauce

SERVES 6

F resh herbs bring out the best in these tender veal chops. The accompanying sauce makes it an authentic Provençale meal.

MARINADE

2 Tbsp.	vegetable oil
½ tsp.	chopped fresh rosemary
½ tsp.	chopped fresh thyme
½ tsp.	minced garlic
½ tsp.	cracked black pepper
6	veal chops

HERBS DE PROVENCE SAUCE

1	medium eggplant
2 Tbsp.	butter
2 Tbsp.	chopped shallots
¼ tsp.	minced garlic
¼ cup	white wine
2	bay leaves
½ cup	whipping cream
¾ cup	demi-glace*
¼ tsp.	chopped fresh thyme
¼ tsp.	chopped fresh rosemary
¼ cup	Dry Sack sherry or dry sherry
½ tsp.	chopped fresh parsley

I n small bowl combine all marinade ingredients; mix well. Season to taste with salt and pepper. Rub veal chops with marinade; cover. Refrigerate 4 hours or overnight.

Heat oven to 300 degrees. Cut eggplant in half; brush each half with oil. Place in roasting pan. Roast, skin side up, 25 to 35 minutes or until tender. Cool. Remove skin; chop pulp finely. In medium saucepan heat 1 Tbsp. butter until hot over medium-high heat; stir in shallots and garlic. Cook until shallots are tender; stir in wine and bay leaves. Reduce heat to medium; cook until wine is reduced by half. Stir in whipping cream, demi-glace, ⅛ tsp. chopped fresh thyme and ⅛ tsp. chopped fresh rosemary. Simmer briefly. Season to taste with salt and pepper; remove bay leaves. In medium frying pan melt remaining 1 Tbsp. butter over medium-high heat; stir in eggplant and remaining herbs. Cook until lightly browned. Stir into sauce; simmer 5 minutes. Keep warm; just before serving stir in sherry and parsley.

Remove veal from marinade; pat dry. Place on broiler pan. Broil 4 to 6 inches from heat 14 to 16 minutes for medium doneness. Serve veal chops with sauce and Dauphinoise potatoes, if desired.

*See Chef's Notes

Tip: Veal chops may be grilled over medium-hot coals until desired doneness.

Stir-Fried Prawns Hong Kong Style

Serves 6

*O*ne doesn't have to travel to the orient to enjoy this stir-fry favorite. A bit of chopping, quick wok cooking, and the meal is complete.

½ tsp.	minced garlic
½ tsp.	minced gingerroot
¼ cup	soy sauce
1½ lb.	uncooked shrimp, peeled, deveined
¼ cup	vegetable oil
½ cup	sliced red bell pepper
½ cup	sliced mushrooms
½ cup	leeks, cut into strips
½ cup	green onions, cut into strips
¼ cup	sliced water chestnuts
¼ cup	oyster sauce
1 Tbsp.	cornstarch
1 Tbsp.	water
4 oz.	snow peas

*M*ix ¼ tsp. garlic, ¼ tsp. gingerroot and 2 Tbsp. soy sauce in medium bowl. Add shrimp; toss to coat. Marinate 20 minutes. Heat oil in wok over high heat until hot. Stir-fry shrimp until they turn pink; remove. In remaining oil in wok stir in red peppers, mushrooms, leeks, green onions and water chestnuts. Stir-fry 2 to 3 minutes or until crisp-tender. Add cooked shrimp, remaining soy sauce and oyster sauce. Mix cornstarch with water, remaining garlic and remaining gingerroot; stir into shrimp mixture. Cook until thickened. Add snow peas; stir-fry until crisp-tender or about 1 minute.

Salmon Coulibiac

Serves 6

A gourmet work of art. The mere appearance of this fine delicacy is satisfying in itself. The taste is out of this world.

Stuffing

2 Tbsp.	olive oil
¼ cup	chopped onion
¼ cup	chopped mushrooms
½ cup	béchamel sauce*
2 cups	spinach, blanched, chopped
8 oz.	cooked fillet of sole, flaked
1	hard cooked egg, chopped
¼ cup	cooked wild rice
½ tsp.	chopped fresh dill
½ tsp.	chopped fresh thyme
¼ tsp.	grated lemon rind
1	(12 oz.) sheet puff pastry
1½ lb.	boneless, skinless salmon fillet
1	egg, well beaten

*H*eat oven to 400 degrees. In medium frying pan heat olive oil over medium-high heat until hot; add onion and mushrooms. Cook until onion is tender. Stir in remaining stuffing ingredients; season to taste with salt and pepper. Continue cooking, stirring occasionally, until stuffing is dry. Cool slightly.

On lightly floured board roll out puff pastry to twice the width of salmon and 2 inches longer. Pastry should be about ⅛-inch thick. Spread half of stuffing down center of pastry; place salmon over pastry folding tail end under. Spread remaining stuffing over salmon. Fold pastry over salmon; pinch seams to seal well. Place seam side down on baking sheet. Brush with beaten egg; prick pastry with fork. Bake 20 minutes or until pastry is golden.

*See Chef's Notes

TENDERLOIN OF BEEF WITH RED WINE MUSHROOM SAUCE

SERVES 6

*T*ry this no-fail recipe on a quality cut of beef, and it will become standard fare for invited dinner guests. All one has to do is vary the accompaniments.

¼ cup	margarine
1 lb.	halved peeled shallots
1 lb.	sliced mushrooms
½ cup	red wine
1 cup	demi-glace*
1 Tbsp.	cracked black peppercorns
2½ lb.	beef tenderloin
1 Tbsp.	cracked black peppercorns

*I*n large frying pan melt margarine over medium-high heat. Stir in shallots and mushrooms. Cook, stirring occasionally, until shallots are almost tender. Stir in wine; cook until wine is reduced by half. Reduce heat to low; stir in demi-glace and peppercorns. Simmer 25 to 30 minutes. Keep warm.

Heat oven to 425 degrees. Rub tenderloin with salt to taste and peppercorns. Place on roasting pan. Roast 35 to 45 minutes or until 140 degrees internal temperature for rare. Remove from oven. Let stand 10 minutes. Slice and serve with mushroom sauce.

*See Chef's Notes

FRUITS DE MER, EN CROUTE

SERVES 6

A compatible combination of shrimp, scallops, mussels and clams come together in this elegant dish. Search for fish-shaped pastry shells to carry out the seafood theme.

¼ cup	clarified butter
¼ cup	chopped onion
½ tsp.	minced garlic
8 oz.	uncooked shrimp, peeled, deveined
8 oz.	scallops
4 oz.	mussels
¼ cup	white wine
½ tsp.	fish base
½ tsp.	shrimp base
2 cups	béchamel sauce*
¼ cup	whipping cream
4 oz.	chopped clams
1 tsp.	chopped parsley
6	baked puff pastry shells, fish shaped if possible

*I*n large frying pan heat butter until hot over medium-high heat. Add onion and garlic; cook until onion is tender. Stir in shrimp, scallops and mussels; cook until shrimp turn pink. Remove seafood from pan. Add wine; cook until wine is reduced by half. Stir fish base and shrimp base into béchamel sauce; heat until sauce is slightly thickened. Stir in cooked seafood and whipping cream; cook until heated through. Add clams; cook just until heated. Stir in parsley; season to taste with salt and pepper. Spoon seafood into puff pastry shells.

*See Chef's Notes

Tip: When preparing béchamel sauce use half-and-half in place of milk.

Sautéed Fillet of Salmon in Pistazio Crust

SERVES 6

The sweet, nutty flavor of this special baked salmon is beyond compare. The glazed fruit topping is outstanding.

¼ cup	sugar
1 Tbsp.	chopped gingerroot
¼ cup	honey
1	grapefruit, peeled, cut into segments
1	orange, peeled, cut into segments
1	lemon, peeled, cut into segments
2 tsp.	Earl Grey tea
1	cup boiling water
2	egg yolks
¼ cup	Kahlua or coffee-flavored liqueur
1	egg white, lightly beaten
6	(6 oz. each) salmon fillets
1 cup	ground toasted pistachio nuts
6	lime leaves, fried
	Grated rind of lime, grapefruit and orange

*I*n small saucepan heat sugar over medium heat until sugar melts and turns golden. Remove from heat, stir in gingerroot and honey. Cook over low heat until gingerroot has flavored glaze. Add hot water if glaze becomes too thick. Strain; cool. Dip fruit segments into ginger glaze; place on waxed paper.

Brew the tea as directed on package for strong tea; cool. In small bowl beat egg yolks, tea and Kahlua. Place in top of double boiler. Cook, whisking constantly until sauce thickens. Keep sauce warm.

Heat oven to 350 degrees. Place egg white in shallow dish; dip salmon in egg white. Coat with pistachios. Bake for 20 to 30 minutes or until fish flakes with a fork.

Place salmon on serving plates. Arrange glazed fruit on salmon; top with lime leaf Sprinkle with zest of lime, grapefruit and orange. Serve with Kahlua sauce.

Bahmi Goreng

SERVES 6

A variegated composition of colors is created in this full-flavored blend of vegetables, meats and seafoods.

1 lb.	uncooked linguine
¼ cup	vegetable oil
½ tsp.	minced garlic
¼ tsp.	minced gingerroot
¼ lb.	diced pork
¼ lb.	diced chicken
½ cup	julienned onion
½ cup	julienned green bell pepper
½ cup	julienned red bell pepper
½ cup	julienned carrots
½ cup	sliced leek
½ cup	shredded cabbage
¼ cup	soy sauce
2 Tbsp.	sambal olek (chili paste)
4 oz.	cooked baby shrimp
1 Tbsp.	sesame oil
¼ cup	chopped green onions

*C*ook linguine according to package directions; drain. Keep warm.

In large frying pan heat vegetable oil until hot over medium-high heat; stir in gingerroot and garlic. Cook until garlic is tender. Add pork and chicken; cook until lightly browned. Add all remaining ingredients except sesame oil, shrimp and green onions. Cook until vegetables are crisp-tender. Stir in hot linguine; toss. Add shrimp and sesame oil; cook just until heated. Season to taste. Garnish with green onions.

SEAFOOD NEWBURG

SERVES 6

This newburg is filled with sweet, succulent lobster, shrimp and scallops. One would be hard pressed to find another as wonderful.

NEWBURG SAUCE

2 Tbsp.	butter
½ cup	chopped celery
¼ cup	chopped onion
1 tsp.	shrimp base
½ tsp.	tomato paste
¼ tsp.	paprika
1	bay leaf
	Dash Worcestershire sauce
	Pinch cayenne pepper
2 cups	fish stock*
2 Tbsp.	roux*
¾ cup	half-and-half
¼ cup	sherry
2 Tbsp.	brandy
½ tsp.	lemon juice
1 Tbsp.	butter
½ cup	chopped onion
4 oz.	uncooked shrimp, peeled, deveined
4 oz.	scallops
1 cup	sliced mushrooms, steamed
4 oz.	cooked lobster meat
½ cup	whipping cream
1½ tsp.	chopped parsley

*I*n medium saucepan melt butter over medium-high heat; stir in celery and onion. Cook until onion is tender. Stir in shrimp base, tomato paste, paprika, bay leaf, Worcestershire sauce and cayenne pepper; cook 1 minute. Stir in stock. Add roux; continue cooking, stirring constantly, until thickened. Add half-and-half; simmer briefly. Stir in 2 Tbsp. sherry, 1 Tbsp. brandy and lemon juice. Strain sauce through cheesecloth. Keep warm.

In large frying pan melt butter over medium-high heat. Stir in onion; cook until tender. Remove onion; set aside. Add shrimp and scallops; cook until shrimp turn pink. Stir in remaining sherry and brandy; stir to remove browned bits. Add cooked onion, Newburg sauce, mushrooms and lobster. Reduce heat to low; simmer 2 to 3 minutes. Stir in whipping cream and parsley.

See Chef's Notes

BAKED MUSHROOM CRÊPES

SERVES 6

There is nothing lovelier to look at than delicate, rolled crêpes. But tasting them surely brings greater pleasure.

¼ cup	butter
2 cups	sliced mushrooms
½ cup	chopped onion
½ tsp.	minced garlic
¼ cup	white wine
1½ cups	béchamel sauce*
½ tsp.	chopped fresh tarragon
½ cup	whipping cream
12	basic crêpes*
1 cup	shredded Cheddar cheese

*H*eat oven to 350 degrees. In large frying pan melt butter over high heat; stir in mushrooms, onion and garlic. Cook until vegetables are tender. Stir in wine; cook until wine is reduced by half. Stir in ¾ cup béchamel sauce and tarragon. Season to taste with salt and pepper. Stir in whipping cream. Divide mushroom mixture among crêpes. Roll crêpes; place in 13×9-inch baking pan. Cover with remaining béchamel sauce; sprinkle with cheese. Bake 15 to 20 minutes or until thoroughly heated and cheese is melted.

See Chef's Notes

GRILLED TENDERLOIN OF PORK WITH SAUTÉED APPLE SLICES

SERVES 6

*S*tart with the black bean mixture first as the beans must be soaked overnight. They become an integral part of this traditional pork and apple combination.

½ lb.	dried black beans
3 Tbsp.	vegetable oil
4	large onions, sliced
4	medium red bell peppers, sliced
4	medium green bell peppers, sliced
3 Tbsp.	chopped fresh thyme
1 tsp.	cumin
1 tsp.	paprika
3 Tbsp.	vegetable oil
1 tsp.	chopped fresh thyme
½ tsp.	minced garlic
¼ tsp.	cracked black peppercorns
3	(10 to 14 oz. each) whole pork tenderloins
3	Granny Smith apples, cored, sliced
2 Tbsp.	chopped cilantro

*P*lace beans in 3-quart saucepan; cover with cold water. Soak overnight; drain. Add 4 cups water; bring to a boil. Cover; reduce heat to low. Cook beans about 1 hour or until tender; drain. Meanwhile, in large frying pan heat oil over medium-high heat until hot. Add onions, peppers, thyme, cumin and paprika. Cook, stirring occasionally until onions are tender. Stir cooked vegetables into beans; season to taste with salt and pepper. Keep warm.

In small bowl mix 2 Tbsp. oil, thyme, garlic and cracked peppercorns. Spread on tenderloins. Cover; refrigerate 4 hours to marinate. Heat oven to 425 degrees. Place tenderloins in roasting pan. Roast 27 to 29 minutes or until internal temperature is 160 degrees for medium doneness.

Let stand 10 minutes. Heat remaining 1 Tbsp. oil in large frying pan; add apple slices. Cook until tender; keep warm. Slice roasts into ½-inch thick slices. Place on serving plates, alternating with apple slices. Stir cilantro and pan juices from roast into black bean mixture. Serve with pork and apples.

PENNE WITH VODKA, TOMATO AND CAVIAR

SERVES 6

*I*talian meets Russian with this sublime, yet simple delicacy.

1 lb.	uncooked penne pasta
½ cup	whipping cream
1¼ cups	basic tomato sauce*
¼ cup	Stolichnaya vodka
1 oz.	caviar
2 Tbsp.	chopped parsley
	Grated Parmesan cheese

*C*ook pasta according to package directions. Drain; keep warm.

In medium saucepan heat cream over medium heat until reduced by half. Stir in tomato sauce; simmer 2 to 3 minutes. Combine pasta with tomato cream sauce; stir in vodka and caviar. Serve in individual pasta bowls. Sprinkle with parsley and Parmesan cheese.

*See Chef's Notes

MENU

THE AMERICAN WAY

*A flag-waving cheer for the Stars and Stripes
marks our salute to the land of pioneer spirit.
From every corner of America comes tasty,
distinctive dishes blending cooking traditions
from all over the world. Tonight, the bounty
of the U.S. and its shining spirit come together
in a star-spangled spectacular!*

═══★═══

GRILLED PORTABELLO MUSHROOM WITH ARUGULA SALAD
FRIED OYSTERS, REMOULADE

═══★═══

CHICKEN AND OKRA SOUP
NAVY BEAN SOUP

═══★═══

SEAFOOD NEWBURG
BLACKENED PORK CHOPS
JAMBALAYA
TENDERLOIN OF BEEF WITH RED WINE MUSHROOM SAUCE

═══★═══

APPLE PIE
BLUEBERRY COBBLER

JAMBALAYA

SERVES 6

*N*ever has there been a more wonderful
combination of seafoods, meats and
vegetables than this popular Cajun dish.
The name itself means a mixture of diverse
elements.

½ cup	bacon fat
1 cup	chopped red bell pepper
1 cup	chopped green bell pepper
1 cup	chopped onion
2 tsp.	minced garlic
½ lb.	uncooked shrimp, shelled, deveined
½ lb.	mussels in shells, scrubbed, beards removed
½ lb.	crayfish, shelled
½ cup	diced ham
2	boneless skinless chicken breasts, cut into 1-inch cubes
2	Andouille sausages, sliced
2½ cups	uncooked rice
5 to 6 cups	chicken stock*
¼ cup	Cajun spices*
¼ cup	gumbo file powder
	Chopped green onions

*I*n 5-quart Dutch oven heat bacon fat over
medium-high heat until hot. Stir in red
and green peppers, onions and garlic;
cook until vegetables are almost tender.
Stir in shrimp, mussels, crayfish, ham,
chicken and sausage; cook until chicken
begins to brown. Stir in rice; cook until
rice is lightly browned. Stir in enough
chicken stock to cover mixture; add
Cajun spices and file powder. Bring to a
boil. Cover; reduce heat to low. Simmer
until rice is tender, about 20 minutes.
Season to taste with salt and pepper.
Garnish with chopped green onions.

*See Chef's Notes

Coquilles Saint Jacques

Serves 6

*T*his recipe always lends an air of style and grace. Perhaps because it is served individually in its own dish. Perhaps because it is luxuriously delicious.

¼ cup	clarified butter
3 cups	fennel, julienned
½	medium onion, julienned
¼ cup	white wine
1½ cups	béchamel sauce*
½ cup	whipping cream
¼ cup	Pernod or anise-flavored liqueur
2 lb.	scallops
½ cup	hollandaise sauce
6	fennel sprigs

*I*n medium frying pan heat 2 Tbsp. clarified butter until hot over medium-high heat; stir in fennel and onion. Cook until crisp-tender. Stir in wine; cook until wine is reduced by half. Stir in béchamel sauce; cook until reduced and thickened. Add whipping cream and 2 Tbsp. Pernod. Season to taste with salt and white pepper. Set aside; keep warm.

In large frying pan heat 2 Tbsp. clarified butter until hot over medium-high heat. Add scallops; cook until scallops turn opaque. Add 2 Tbsp. Pernod; season to taste with salt and pepper. Divide fennel mixture into 6 oven-proof dishes; top with scallops. Spoon hollandaise sauce over each. Broil 2 to 3 inches from heat 2 to 3 minutes or until lightly browned. Garnish each with fennel sprig.

See Chef's Notes

Grilled New Zealand Lamb Chops

Serves 6

*A*n exciting combination of fresh mint, cilantro, garlic and cracked pepper yield a flavorful paste that's broiled into the chops.

2 Tbsp.	vegetable oil
1 Tbsp.	chopped fresh mint
1 Tbsp.	chopped cilantro
1 tsp.	minced garlic
½ tsp.	cracked black peppercorns
18	french-cut lamb chops

CURRIED RATATOUILLE

2 Tbsp.	vegetable oil
¼ cup	chopped onion
2	bay leaves
½ tsp.	Madras curry powder
½ cup	finely chopped tomato
½ cup	chopped zucchini
½ cup	chopped eggplant
½ cup	finely chopped red bell pepper
½ cup	chopped yellow squash
1 cup	cooked navy beans
¼ cup	coconut milk

*I*n food processor, blend oil, mint, cilantro, garlic, peppercorns and salt to taste into paste. Spread paste evenly on both sides of lamb chops. Cover; refrigerate 4 hours.

In medium saucepan heat vegetable oil over medium-high heat until hot; stir in onion and bay leaves. Cook until onion is tender and golden brown. Add curry powder; cook 1 minute. Stir in tomatoes; cook 5 minutes, stirring occasionally. Stir in zucchini, eggplant, red pepper and yellow squash. Cook until vegetables are tender and flavors are blended. Stir in navy beans and coconut milk. Season to taste with salt and pepper. Remove bay leaves.

Place lamb chops on broiler pan. Broil 4 to 6 inches from heat for 7 to 11 minutes, turning once for medium doneness. Spoon ⅙ of ratatouille into center of individual serving plates; surround with 3 lamb chops.

CHURRASCO

SERVES 6

O nce prepared, reserve half of the chimichurri to serve with the grilled steak. This recipe suggests adding the sweet taste of glazed jicama on the side. It's quite nice.

CHIMICHURRI

½ cup   chopped onion
¼ cup   chopped parsley
¼ cup   chopped cilantro
¼ cup   white wine
¼ cup   olive oil
2 Tbsp.   minced garlic
1 Tbsp.   cracked pepper
1 tsp.   chopped fresh thyme

6   (8 oz. each) skirt steaks

¼ cup   margarine
1 Tbsp.   sugar
1 ½ lb.   jicama, julienned
2 Tbsp.   cornstarch
2 Tbsp.   chopped cilantro

P lace all ingredients for chimichurri in food processor bowl fitted with metal blade; process until finely chopped. Reserve half of mixture to serve with broiled steaks. Cover; chill. In remaining mixture marinate steaks at least 6 hours in refrigerator. Place steaks on broiler pan. Broil 4 to 6 inches from heat until desired doneness, about 12 minutes for medium, turning once.

In large frying pan melt margarine over high heat. Stir in sugar; cook until sugar is melted and golden. Stir in jicama; stir to coat. Cook until jicama is glazed. Dissolve cornstarch in 2 Tbsp. water; stir into jicama. Cook, stirring constantly, until liquid is thickened. Stir in cilantro. Serve glazed jicama and reserved chimichurri with broiled steaks.

Tip: Steaks can be cooked over medium coals on a charcoal grill.

PASTA WITH SUN-DRIED TOMATOES AND SMOKED TURKEY

SERVES 4

T his northern Italian white sauce invites a hint of sun-dried tomatoes to balance the smoky flavor of the turkey.

8 oz.   uncooked fettucine pasta
4 oz.   sun-dried tomatoes
3 Tbsp.   butter, softened
¼ cup   chopped shallots
3   cloves garlic, minced
¾ cup   glace de poulet*
½ cup   white wine
2 cups   whipping cream
6 oz.   smoked turkey, julienned
2 Tbsp.   fresh basil, chiffonade

Grated Parmesan cheese
Basil leaves

C ook pasta according to package directions. Drain; keep warm.

In small bowl cover sun-dried tomatoes with hot water; let stand. When softened pour off water; cut into julienne strips. In medium saucepan melt 1 Tbsp. butter over medium-high heat. Add shallots and garlic; cook until shallots are tender. Stir in glace de poulet and white wine. Continue cooking until liquid is reduced by half. Stir in whipping cream; cook until cream is reduced by half. Stir in smoked turkey and sun-dried tomatoes; simmer 2 minutes. Remove from heat; whisk in remaining butter. Stir in basil; season to taste with salt and pepper. Toss sauce and pasta. Garnish with grated Parmesan cheese and basil leaves.

*See Chef's Notes

Stuffed Chicken Leg with Langoustine Tail

Serves 6

*O*nce deboned, chicken legs make a nice showcase for this mousse stuffing. The langoustine and corn and pepper pancakes create an inviting plate.

Chicken Mousse

1½ lb.	boneless skinless chicken breasts
3	egg whites
2½ cups	whipping cream
¼ cup	goat cheese, creamed
1 tsp.	minced gingerroot
6	medium-sized chicken legs
6 Tbsp.	unsalted butter
¼ cup	chopped shallots
12 oz.	mushrooms, finely chopped
1 Tbsp.	chopped fresh tarragon
1 Tbsp.	chopped fresh thyme
1 Tbsp.	chopped fresh chives
30	langoustine (prawn) tails, shelled
3 cups	vegetable stock*
3 Tbsp.	olive oil
6	lobster heads
2 Tbsp.	chopped onion
1 Tbsp.	chopped carrot
1 Tbsp.	chopped celery
1	cloves garlic, minced
¼ cup	brandy
1 Tbsp.	tomato paste
½ cup	chicken stock*
¼ cup	sherry
1¼ cups	whipping cream

Corn and Pepper Pancakes

¼ cup	butter
⅓ cup	chopped red bell pepper
⅓ cup	chopped green bell pepper
½ cup	all-purpose flour
½ cup	+ 2 Tbsp. whipping cream
5	egg yolks
1½ cups	corn
½ cup	vegetable oil
12	chives tops

*M*ince chicken breast by hand or in blender. Place fine sieve over small bowl; set bowl over ice. Press chicken through sieve. In mixer bowl beat egg whites until soft peaks form. Over ice fold whites into chicken; stir until mixture becomes very stiff. Over ice slowly add cream, stirring constantly. Stir in goat cheese and gingerroot; season to taste with salt and pepper. Refrigerate until needed.

Bone out chicken leg easing flesh away from bone. Start at thigh and work way down to drumstick. Do not pierce skin. Refrigerate until needed.

In small frying pan melt butter over high heat; add shallots. Cook until tender. Add mushrooms; cook until all liquid is evaporated. Cool completely. Stir mushroom mixture and herbs into chicken mousse; mix well.

Cook langoustine tails in vegetable stock for 2 minutes. Drain; cool in ice water. Cut 12 cooked tails into small pieces. Stir into chicken mousse.

Heat oven to 375 degrees. Place 2 Tbsp. olive oil and 1 Tbsp. butter in roasting pan. Rub inside of chicken leg with salt and pepper. Pipe chicken mousse into legs; sew closed with fine string. Coat stuffed legs with fat. Roast until golden brown, basting occasionally. Drain off fat.

In medium saucepan heat 1 Tbsp. olive oil over high heat; stir in lobster heads. Cook until lightly browned. Add onion, carrot, celery and garlic; cook until tender. Add brandy; ignite carefully. Stir in tomato paste, chicken broth and 2 Tbsp. sherry. Reduce heat to medium; simmer 20 minutes, skimming frequently. Strain sauce through cheesecloth. Stir in cream; continue cooking until sauce is reduced and thickened. Stir in remaining sherry and remaining butter. Season to taste with salt and pepper; add reserved langoustine tails. Cook until warmed through; keep warm.

In small frying pan melt butter over medium-high heat; add red and green peppers. Cook until tender; drain well. In medium bowl combine flour, cream and egg yolks; whisk until smooth. Stir in corn and peppers; season to taste with salt and pepper. In large frying pan heat oil with 2 Tbsp. butter until hot. Shape pancakes 2 inches in diameter and about ½ inch thick. Fry in oil mixture until browned, turning once. Keep warm.

Place chicken leg on plate; spoon sauce over. Garnish with 3 langoustine tails and 2 chive tops. Serve with corn and pepper pancakes.

See Chef's Notes

OAK SMOKED PORK LOIN WITH CHAMPAGNE CABBAGE

SERVES 6

*T*he sweet honey and pineapple glaze over smoked pork proves that opposites do attract. The ¼ cup of bubbly makes this cabbage recipe delicious. Uniquely delicious.

1 cup	thinly sliced onions
½ cup	all-purpose flour
	Oil for frying
½ cup	pineapple juice
¼ cup	honey
1 Tbsp.	Coleman's mustard
2½ lb.	smoked fully cooked pork loin

CHAMPAGNE CABBAGE

1 Tbsp.	duck fat or butter
1 Tbsp.	sugar
4 cups	coarsely chopped cabbage
¼ tsp.	caraway seeds
¼ cup	champagne
1½ tsp.	cornstarch
1 Tbsp.	water

*C*oat onions in flour. Fry in hot oil until crisp; drain. Keep warm.

Heat oven to 350 degrees. In small bowl, combine pineapple juice, honey and mustard; mix well. Brush honey mixture generously over pork. Bake for 20 to 30 minutes or until glazed and heated through. Slice and keep warm.

Meanwhile, melt duck fat in large frying pan; stir in sugar. Cook over medium-high heat until sugar melts and turns golden. Stir in cabbage; cook until cabbage begins to soften. Stir in caraway seeds. Reduce heat to medium. Cover; cook 10 to 15 minutes or until cabbage is crisp-tender. Stir in champagne; season to taste with salt and white pepper. Dissolve cornstarch in water. Stir into cabbage mixture; cook until sauce has thickened.

Serve sliced pork with cabbage; garnish with fried onions.

SUPREME DE POULET FARCIE

SERVES 6

A rich, tarragon wine sauce adds the finishing touch to this exceptional stuffed chicken.

2 tsp.	margarine
¼ cup	chopped onion
½ tsp.	minced garlic
1	(10 oz.) pkg. frozen chopped spinach, thawed, squeezed dry
¼ cup	grated Swiss cheese
6	skinless boneless chicken breast halves
½ cup	all-purpose flour
1 Tbsp.	chopped fresh tarragon
1 to 2 Tbsp.	vegetable oil
1 cup	chicken stock or broth*

TARRAGON SAUCE

¼ cup	butter, softened
2 Tbsp.	chopped shallots
½ tsp.	minced garlic
1	bay leaf
½ cup	white wine
1 cup	glace de poulet*
½ cup	whipping cream
1 cup	béchamel sauce*
1 Tbsp.	chopped fresh tarragon

Heat oven to 350 degrees. In medium skillet melt margarine over medium-high heat; stir in onions and garlic. Cook until onions are tender; stir in spinach. Continue cooking 1 to 2 minutes; remove from heat. Cool. Stir Swiss cheese into spinach mixture. Carefully pound chicken breasts to flatten. Divide spinach mixture evenly among chicken breasts. Roll up breasts, enclosing filling. Secure with wooden picks. In shallow dish mix flour and tarragon; season to taste with salt and pepper. Roll stuffed breasts in flour mixture. Heat oil in non-stick frying pan over medium-high heat; add chicken and brown on all sides. Place browned breasts in baking pan; pour stock over each breast. Cover; bake for

15 to 20 minutes or until chicken is no longer pink in center.

In medium saucepan, melt 2 Tbsp. butter over medium-high heat; stir in shallots, garlic and bay leaf. Cook until shallots are tender; stir in white wine. Continue cooking until wine is reduced by half. Reduce heat to medium. Stir in glace de poulet and whipping cream; simmer briefly. Add béchamel sauce; simmer 5 minutes. Stir in fresh tarragon; remove bay leaf. Keep warm. Whisk remaining 2 Tbsp. butter into sauce just before serving.

Serve stuffed chicken breasts with Tarragon Sauce.

* See Chef's Notes

TROUT ALMONDINE

SERVES 6

I magine pan frying the day's catch over an open fire next to a trout stream. Here's how to achieve the same taste in a metropolitan high rise.

½ cup	butter
1 cup	slivered almonds
½ cup	all-purpose flour
6	trout (boneless and headless)
	Vegetable oil
2 Tbsp.	chopped parsley

In small saucepan over high heat melt butter; stir in almonds. Cook, stirring constantly until almonds turn golden brown. Remove from heat; keep warm.

In shallow dish combine flour and salt and pepper to taste. Open up trout; coat both sides with flour. In large frying pan heat oil until hot over medium-high heat. Add trout; cook until trout flakes with a fork, turning once. Spoon almond butter over trout; sprinkle with parsley.

Jumbo Shrimp Fra Diavolo

SERVES 6

The flavor of most pasta and sauce recipes is imparted in the sauce. This unique taste is broiled right into the shrimp.

1 lb. uncooked fresh fettucine

½ tsp. minced garlic
¼ tsp. chopped fresh rosemary
¼ tsp. Coleman's mustard
⅛ tsp. crushed red pepper flakes
24 uncooked jumbo shrimp, peeled tail on, deveined

SAUCE

2 Tbsp. olive oil
½ cup red pepper coulis*
¼ tsp. minced garlic
2 cups basic tomato sauce*
⅛ tsp. crushed red pepper flakes

In large saucepan cook fettucine according to package directions. Drain; keep warm.

In small bowl mix ½ tsp. garlic, rosemary, mustard and red pepper. Spread on shrimp; marinate 20 minutes.

In medium saucepan heat olive oil until hot over medium-high heat; stir in red pepper coulis and ¼ tsp. garlic. Cook until garlic is tender. Stir in tomato sauce and ⅛ tsp. red pepper; simmer briefly. Season to taste with salt.

Place shrimp on broiler pan. Broil 4 to 6 inches from heat 4 to 5 minutes or until shrimp turn pink. Add shrimp to sauce. Toss sauce with cooked fettucine.

See Chef's Notes

Breast of Duck with Raspberry Coulis

SERVES 12

Duck has always been a highlight on fine dining menus. None could be more outstanding than this remarkable rendition.

24 boneless skinless duck breast halves
½ cup red wine
¼ cup raspberry puree
1 Tbsp. vegetable oil

RASPBERRY COULIS

4 cups raspberry puree
1 cup chicken stock*
2 Tbsp. sugar
2 Tbsp. balsamic vinegar
1½ tsp. black peppercorns

Place duck breast in food storage bag. In small bowl combine red wine, raspberry puree and oil; season to taste with salt and pepper. Add to duck; seal bag. Toss to coat duck. Refrigerate overnight.

In medium saucepan combine ingredients for raspberry coulis; bring to a boil over medium-high heat. Reduce heat to low; simmer 5 minutes. Remove from heat; strain through cheesecloth. If coulis is too thin, thicken with cornstarch dissolved in chicken stock or water; keep warm.

Remove duck from marinade; pat dry. Place on broiler pan. Broil 4 to 6 inches from heat 8 to 12 minutes or until desired doneness, turning once. Serve over raspberry coulis.

See Chef's Notes

Tip: Duck may be cooked over medium-hot coals until desired doneness. Mark with crisscross pattern from grill while grilling.

"LORD WELLINGTON" BAKED TENDERLOIN OF BEEF

SERVES 10

*I*t was generous of the Duke of Wellington to share this marvelous creation. This particular version is decidedly different with the addition of truffle pâte.

1	(about 3½ lb.) beef tenderloin
½ cup	margarine
2 lb.	chopped mushrooms
1 cup	finely chopped onion
2	bay leaves
½ lb.	truffle pâte
	Puff pastry sheet
1	egg, well beaten
2 drops	yellow food color

SAUCE PERIGOURDINE

1 cup	demi-glace*
2 Tbsp.	truffle pâte
¼ cup	red wine
2 Tbsp.	brandy

*H*eat oven to 450 degrees. Heat large nonstick frying pan over high heat until hot; add beef. Cook until browned on all sides. Remove; set aside. Add margarine, mushrooms and onions to frying pan; cook until onion is tender and mushrooms cooked. Continue cooking until any liquid is evaporated. Cool; mix in pâte. Spread pâte mixture over top of beef. On lightly floured board roll puff pastry into rectangle twice as wide as beef and 2 inches longer. Pastry should be ⅛-inch thick. Place beef in center; roll pastry enclosing beef. Pinch seams to seal; place on baking sheet. In small bowl mix egg with food color; brush over pastry. Prick pastry with fork every 4 inches. Bake 10 minutes or until pastry is firm. Reduce heat to 350 degrees. Continue baking until internal temperature is 120 degrees. Remove from oven; let stand 10 minutes before slicing.

In small saucepan heat demi-glace over low heat. In small bowl mix pâte with wine and brandy until smooth. Remove demi-glace from heat; whisk in pate. Do not allow sauce to boil or it will separate. Serve beef with warm sauce.

*See Chef's Notes

Tip: Truffle pâte is available at some supermarkets and gourmet cooking stores.

BROILED BEEF-BULGOGI

SERVES 4

*I*n Korea, bulgogi is grilled right at the table. It is a favorite around the world served with rice and side salad.

1 lb.	lean beef
2 Tbsp.	soy sauce
1 Tbsp.	sugar
1 Tbsp.	sesame oil
1 Tbsp.	salt
⅛ tsp.	pepper
1 Tbsp.	water or rice wine
4	green onions, chopped
3	cloves garlic, minced

*C*ut beef into 3-inch squares about ⅛-inch thick. In small bowl combine all ingredients except beef; mix well. Pour into food storage bag; add beef strips. Seal bag; toss to coat beef with marinade. Refrigerate up to 1½ hours before cooking. Place beef on broiler pan. Broil 4 to 6 inches from heat 3 to 5 minutes or until beef is cooked to desired doneness, turning once.

Tip: Traditionally this meat is broiled at the table on a Korean bulgogi charcoal grill or hot plate.

GRILLED VEAL CHOPS OVER FINE HERB GALETTE WITH CRACKED CORIANDER PORT WINE REDUCTION

SERVES 6

The herb galette is brimming with flavor. And the port wine sauce delivers outstanding goodness without overpowering.

6	(8 oz. each) veal chops, Frenched
2 Tbsp.	olive oil
1½ tsp.	chopped fresh thyme
1½ tsp.	chopped fresh oregano
1½ tsp.	cracked black pepper

FINE HERB GALETTE

18 slices	white bread, crust removed
¼ cup	beef stock*
2 Tbsp.	clarified butter
¼ cup	chopped onions
⅛ cup	chopped celery
¼ tsp.	minced garlic
1	bay leaf
3	egg yolks
3 Tbsp.	milk
¼ cup	sliced mushrooms
¼ cup	dried porcini mushrooms, soaked, chopped
1½ tsp.	porcini powder
½ tsp.	chopped fresh oregano
½ tsp.	chopped fresh thyme
½ tsp.	cracked black pepper

PORT WINE REDUCTION

2 Tbsp.	coriander seeds
2 Tbsp.	clarified butter
¼ cup	chopped shallots
¼ tsp.	minced garlic
½ cup	port wine
½ cup	glaze de viande
½ cup	demi-glace*

Place veal chops in food storage bag. In small bowl combine olive oil, herbs, pepper and salt to taste. Add to veal; seal bag. Toss to coat veal; marinate in refrigerator 4 hours.

Cut bread into medium-size squares; place in medium bowl. Mix bread with beef stock; set aside. In small frying pan heat butter over high heat until hot. Add onion, celery, garlic and bay leaf; cook until onion is tender. Remove bay leaf. In small bowl mix egg yolks and milk. Add onion mixture and all remaining ingredients to bread; mix well. Grease a 12×14-inch sheet of aluminum foil. Spoon bread along long edge of foil forming log about 2½-inches in diameter; roll tightly. Be sure all seams are sealed. Steam for 20 to 25 minutes. Cool; remove foil. Cut into 6 slices. Keep warm.

In small pan over high heat toast coriander seeds; crack in spice grinder. In medium saucepan heat butter until hot over medium-high heat; add shallots and garlic. Cook until shallots are tender. Add port wine; cook until wine is reduced by half. Add coriander, glaze de viande and demi-glace. Reduce heat to low; simmer 15 minutes. Keep warm.

Remove veal chops from marinade; place on broiler pan. Broil 4 to 6 inches from heat 14 to 16 minutes or until desired doneness, turning once. On serving plates place veal chop over herb galette; serve with sauce.

See Chef's Notes

TROPICAL COCONUT SEAFOOD

SERVES 6

*W*hat a pleasant way to enjoy the abundance of the sea. Here a selection of seafoods comes together in an excellent sauce.

SOFRITO

1 cup	chopped onion
1 cup	chopped green bell pepper
1 cup	chopped red bell pepper
2 cups	chopped tomatoes
6	cloves garlic, peeled
1	jalapeño pepper, chopped
¼ cup	olive oil

COCONUT-LIME SAUCE

1 cup	fish stock*
1 cup	coconut milk
½ cup	chopped tomato
1½ tsp.	instant fish bouillon
1 Tbsp.	lime juice
¼ cup	roux*
2 Tbsp.	water
¼ cup	chopped cilantro

1 Tbsp.	margarine
6 oz.	shrimp, peeled, deveined
6 oz.	scallops
6 oz.	firm fish fillet, chopped
4 oz.	mussel meat
4 oz.	whole clams
½ cup	whipping cream

Timbale of saffron rice

*H*eat oven to 300 degrees. In roasting pan combine sofrito ingredients. Bake 45 minutes or until all vegetables are soft. Place in food processor bowl fitted with metal blade. Process until smooth.

In medium saucepan combine fish stock and coconut milk. Heat over medium-high heat until reduced by half. Stir in ¾ cup sofrito, tomatoes, fish bouillon and lime juice. Reduce heat to low; simmer several minutes. Mix roux with water until smooth; stir into sauce. Continue cooking, stirring constantly, until

thickened. Stir in cilantro. Keep warm.

In large frying pan melt margarine over medium-high heat. Add seafood; cook until shrimp turn pink. Do not overcook. Remove seafood; set aside. Continue cooking until juices are reduced. Stir in 2½ cups coconut-lime sauce; cook until hot. Add cooked seafood and cream. Season to taste with salt and pepper. On individual serving plates ladle seafood around timbale of saffron rice.

*See Chef's Notes

FRESH CATCH OF THE DAY PAN FRIED WITH ROSEMARY & ROASTED GARLIC BEURRE NOISETTE

SERVES 6

*T*he roasted garlic and fresh rosemary are what elevate a simple seafood dinner to an extraordinarily special meal.

GARLIC BEURRE NOISETTE

2 Tbsp.	garlic slivers
¼ cup	clarified butter
½ tsp.	chopped fresh rosemary

½ cup	all-purpose flour
1 Tbsp.	paprika
6	(6 oz. each) grouper or snapper fillets
¼ cup	butter

*H*eat oven to 400 degrees. Place garlic in small baking dish; bake 5 to 10 minutes or until golden brown, stirring occasionally. Place roasted garlic and clarified butter in small saucepan. Cook over low heat until moisture has evaporated from garlic. Stir in rosemary; keep warm.

In shallow dish combine flour, paprika and salt and pepper to taste. Coat fish fillets with flour mixture. In large frying pan melt butter over medium-high heat until hot. Cook fish in butter until it flakes with a fork, turning once. Serve fish with Garlic Beurre Noisette.

*See Chef's Notes

New Sirloin Steak "Martinique"

SERVES 6

A creamy wine and mushroom sauce is the perfect complement to this popular American cut of steak. Charcoal grilling adds a great outdoor taste.

6	(10 oz. each) New York strip loin steaks
	Vegetable oil
	Cracked peppercorns
	Bay leaf, broken
1 Tbsp.	butter
2 Tbsp.	finely chopped onion
½ tsp.	minced garlic
1 cup	sliced mushrooms, blanched
2 tsp.	cracked peppercorns
¼ cup	red wine
2 Tbsp.	brandy
1 cup	demi-glace*
½ cup	whipping cream

Brush steaks with oil, sprinkle with peppercorns and bay leaves. Refrigerate until cooking time. In small saucepan melt butter over high heat until melted; stir in onion and garlic. Cook until tender. Stir in mushrooms, peppercorns, wine and brandy. Reduce heat to low; cook until sauce is reduced by half. Add demi-glace; simmer 5 minutes. Stir in cream; season to taste with salt and pepper. Keep warm.

Remove bay leaves from steaks; place steaks on broiler pan. Broil 2 to 4 inches from heat about 12 minutes for medium, turning once. Season with salt; serve with sauce.

*See Chef's Notes

Tip: Steaks can be cooked over medium coals on a charcoal grill.

Madras Vegetable Curry

SERVES 6

An assortment of distinctive spices make this Indian vegetable dish dance with tremendous flavor.

2 Tbsp.	vegetable oil
½ cup	chopped onion
4	whole cloves
4	cardamom pods
1	cinnamon stick
½ tsp.	minced garlic
½ tsp.	gingerroot
1 Tbsp.	Madras curry powder
½ cup	diced tomatoes
2	bay leaves
½ cup	diced potatoes
½ cup	chopped carrot
½ cup	chopped cauliflower
½ cup	diced eggplant
½ cup	coconut milk
½ cup	peas
¼ cup	chopped cilantro

Cooked rice flavored with cinnamon

In large frying pan heat oil until hot over medium-high heat. Stir in onion, cloves, cinnamon and cardamom. Cook until onion begins to brown. Stir in garlic, ginger, and curry powder; cook until flavors are released. Add tomatoes and bay leaves; cook 3 minutes. Reduce heat to low; stir in potatoes. Continue cooking 5 to 6 minutes or until potatoes are partially cooked. Stir in carrot, cauliflower, eggplant and coconut milk. Simmer until vegetables are tender, stirring occasionally. Remove bay leaves and whole spices. Stir in peas. Season to taste with salt; stir in cilantro. Serve with cooked rice flavored with cinnamon.

Jerk Cornish Hen

SERVES 6

A 24-hour marinade is the secret to this flavorful, juicy entree. The combination of vegetables, herbs and spices makes it uncommonly good.

1 cup	chopped carrots
1 cup	chopped onion
½ cup	chopped green onions
¼ cup	chopped celery
2 Tbsp.	vegetable oil
2 Tbsp.	soy sauce
2 Tbsp.	vinegar
1 tsp.	hot pepper sauce
¾ tsp.	minced garlic
½ tsp.	cracked black pepper
½ tsp.	jerk seasoning
¼ tsp.	chopped fresh thyme
	Pinch of grated nutmeg
6	Cornish hens, split in center

*I*n medium bowl combine all ingredients except Cornish hens; mix well. Rub mixture into each hen; pour any remaining mixture over hens. Cover; refrigerate. Let hens marinate for 24 hours.

Remove hens from marinade; pat dry. Heat oven to 350 degrees. Place hens in roasting pan. Roast until internal temperature is 160 degrees.

Tip: Hens can also be grilled over low coals on a charcoal grill.

Tournedos of Beef Tenderloin

SERVES 6

*T*he béarnaise requires the most attention with tournedos of beef. But it's definitely worth the effort.

BÉARNAISE SAUCE

½ cup	red wine vinegar
½ cup	chopped onion
2 tsp.	chopped fresh tarragon
½ tsp.	minced garlic
½ tsp.	cracked black peppercorns
3	egg yolks
1 cup	clarified butter
1 Tbsp.	chopped parsley
¼ cup	margarine
1 lb.	quartered mushrooms
¼ cup	chopped onion
2	bay leaves
1 Tbsp.	chopped parsley
1½ lb.	beef tenderloin, sliced into 12 slices
3	medium tomatoes, halved, seeded

*I*n medium saucepan heat vinegar, onion, tarragon, garlic and peppercorns over high heat until reduced by half; strain. Place egg yolks in top of double boiler; whisk until thickened slightly and pale yellow. Place double boiler over low heat, whisking yolks constantly until yolks have thickened and bottom of pan is visible between strokes. Remove from heat; slowly whisk in clarified butter, drop by drop. Stir in vinegar reduction and parsley. Keep warm over warm water.

In large frying pan melt margarine over high heat; stir in mushrooms, onion and bay leaves. Cook, stirring constantly, until onion is tender. Remove bay leaves. Season to taste with salt and pepper; stir in parsley. Keep warm.

Place beef on broiler pan. Broil 4 inches from heat 8 to 12 minutes, turning once, or until desired doneness. Place on serving plates; add mushrooms to each. Spoon Béarnaise sauce into tomato halves; serve with beef

* See Chef's Notes

Tip: Beef can be cooked over hot coals on a charcoal grill.

ANCHO HONEY BASTED ATLANTIC SALMON

SERVES 6

Out of the depths of the cold Atlantic comes this delicate seafood. Serve it over a Five Bean Salad that is as colorful as it is delicious.

4	ancho chiles
2 Tbsp.	honey
1½ Tbsp.	orange juice concentrate
1 Tbsp.	balsamic vinegar
¼ tsp.	salt
¼ tsp.	minced garlic
1 tsp.	Cointreau or orange-flavored liqueur
6	(6 oz. each) pieces salmon fillet

FIVE BEAN SALAD

1 cup	chopped tomatoes
½ cup	chopped onion
½ cup	chopped green onions
⅓ cup	cooked pinto beans
⅓ cup	cooked black-eyed peas
⅓ cup	cooked navy beans
⅓ cup	cooked red beans
⅓ cup	cooked black beans
¼ cup	chopped green bell pepper
¼ cup	chopped red bell pepper
¼ cup	chopped cilantro
¼ cup	olive oil
1 tsp.	minced garlic
	Pinch ground cumin

In small bowl soak chiles in warm water. When softened, remove seeds. Place chiles, honey, orange juice concentrate, vinegar, salt, garlic and Cointreau in blender container. Blend until chiles are finely chopped. Pat salmon dry; spread with chile paste. Place on broiler pan. Broil 4 to 6 inches from heat 10 to 15 minutes or until salmon flakes with a fork.

Meanwhile, in medium bowl combine all ingredients for Five Bean Salad; mix well.

Serve salmon over Five Bean Salad.

PENNE MARISCOS

SERVES 6

Saffron, the most expensive spice in the world, makes this pasta dish a real treasure. Indeed, a royal taste sensation.

2 lb.	uncooked penne pasta
¼ cup	butter
¼ cup	chopped onion
2	bay leaves
2 cups	fish stock*
	Pinch saffron
1 cup	half-and-half
1 Tbsp.	roux*
¼ cup	whipping cream
¼ cup	Pernod liqueur or anise-flavored liqueur
1 lb.	scallops
1 lb.	uncooked shrimp, peeled, deveined
6 oz.	lobster meat
6	sprigs fennel leaves

Cook pasta according to package directions. Drain; keep warm.

In medium saucepan melt 2 Tbsp. butter over medium-high heat; stir in onion and bay leaves. Cook until onion is tender. Stir in fish stock and saffron; simmer about 10 minutes or until saffron has colored and flavored sauce. Stir in half-and-half; simmer 5 minutes. Whisk in roux; cook, stirring constantly, until sauce is thickened. Stir in 2 Tbsp. whipping cream; simmer 2 minutes. Season to taste with salt and white pepper; stir in Pernod. Keep warm.

In large frying pan melt remaining butter over medium-high heat. Add scallops; cook until juices are sealed in. Stir in shrimp and lobster; cook until shrimp turn pink. Remove seafood; drain liquid. Pour liquid back into frying pan; cook until reduced by half. Stir in saffron sauce; simmer 3 to 5 minutes. Stir in seafood and pasta; cook until heated through. Just before serving stir in remaining whipping cream and additional Pernod to taste. Garnish with fennel sprigs.

*See Chef's Notes

HUNAN FILET OF BEEF

SERVES 6

Orange aficionados will rave over this Asian beef tenderloin. The coconut-braised Chinese cabbage makes a fascinating side dish.

1 Tbsp.	vegetable oil
½ tsp.	minced garlic
½ tsp.	chopped gingerroot
3 Tbsp.	frozen orange juice concentrate, thawed
1 Tbsp.	Cointreau or orange-flavored liqueur
2 Tbsp.	soy sauce
2 lb.	beef tenderloin roast

ORANGE GLAZE

1½ tsp.	sugar
1 cup	orange juice
¼ cup	chopped shallots
1 cup	demi-glace*
1 Tbsp.	butter, softened

COCONUT-BRAISED CABBAGE

2 Tbsp.	margarine
½ cup	chopped onion
2	bay leaves
3 cups	sliced Chinese cabbage
1 cup	coconut milk
1 Tbsp.	cornstarch
¼ cup	chopped green onions

In small frying pan heat oil over medium-high heat until hot. Stir in garlic and gingerroot; cook until garlic is tender. Stir in soy sauce and orange juice concentrate; bring to a boil. Remove from heat; stir in Cointreau. Cool completely. Pour marinade over beef. Cover; refrigerate 2 hours.

In small saucepan heat sugar over medium-high heat until melted and golden. Stir in orange juice and shallots. Continue cooking until juice is reduced by half. Stir in demi-glace. Reduce heat to low; simmer 20 to 25 minutes. Whisk in butter; keep warm.

In medium saucepan melt margarine over medium-high heat; stir in onion and bay leaves. Cook until onion is tender. Stir in Chinese cabbage; cook until cabbage begins to wilt. Add coconut milk; continue cooking until cabbage is crisp-tender and milk is reduced. In small bowl mix cornstarch with 1 Tbsp. water. Stir into cabbage mixture; cook, stirring constantly, until thickened. Season to taste with salt and pepper; remove bay leaves. Stir in green onions.

Heat oven to 425 degrees. Remove beef from marinade; pat dry. Place in roasting pan. Roast 35 to 45 minutes for medium, or until desired doneness.

Serve beef with Orange Glaze and Coconut-Braised Cabbage.

*See Chef's Notes

VEAL PARMESAN

SERVES 6

A long-standing favorite. All great chefs have a version of this in their repertoire.

½ cup	all-purpose flour
6	(4 oz. each) veal cutlets, pounded ¼-inch thick
2	eggs, well beaten
½ cup	dried bread crumbs
2 Tbsp.	vegetable oil
1½ cups	basic tomato sauce*
1½ cups	shredded mozzarella cheese

Heat oven to 300 degrees. In shallow dish combine flour with salt and pepper to taste. Dip cutlets in flour and then in egg. Coat with bread crumbs. In large frying pan heat oil over medium heat until hot; add cutlets. Cook 3 to 4 minutes or until desired doneness, turning once. Place cutlets in 13×9-inch baking pan. Cover with tomato sauce and mozzarella cheese. Bake 15 to 20 minutes or until heated through and cheese is melted.

*See Chef's Notes

BRAISED SALMON WITH ROQUEFORT AND CELERY

SERVES 6

*S*callop mousse graces the outer layer of each salmon fillet. The Roquefort and celery wine sauce is utterly divine.

WHITE WINE SAUCE

6 Tbsp.	dry white wine
1 tsp.	chopped shallots
8	white peppercorns, cracked
¾ cup	+ 2 Tbsp. fish stock*
6 Tbsp.	vegetable stock*
6 Tbsp.	whipping cream
	Cayenne pepper
2 Tbsp.	unsalted butter
¼ cup	celery leaves
¼ cup	crumbled Roquefort or blue cheese
½ cup	julienned celery, blanched

SCALLOP MOUSSE

1½ lb.	scallops
2	egg whites
1 cup	whipping cream
6	(6 oz. each) salmon fillets
2 Tbsp.	minced fresh chives and tarragon
½ cup	fresh white bread crumbs
6 Tbsp.	unsalted butter
6	sprigs celery leaves, fried
6	fleurons

*I*n small saucepan combine wine, shallots and peppercorns; cook over medium-high heat until reduced by two-thirds. Stir in fish stock and vegetable stock and reduce by two-thirds. Add whipping cream and reduce by half. Season to taste with salt and cayenne pepper. In small frying pan melt 2 Tbsp. butter; add celery leaves. Cook until tender over medium-heat; stir into white wine sauce. Reduce heat to low; simmer 10 minutes. Press through sieve; stir in cheese and julienned celery. Keep warm.

Season scallops with salt and pepper; refrigerate 1 hour. Pat scallops dry; mince by hand or in blender. Place fine sieve over a small bowl; set bowl over ice. Press scallops through sieve. In mixer bowl beat egg whites on high speed until soft peaks form. Over ice fold whites into scallops. Over ice slowly add cream; mix until well blended.

Season salmon to taste with salt and pepper. Mix scallop mousse with herbs; press through sieve. Spread thin layer of mousse over salmon; wrap in plastic wrap. Place in steamer over boiling water; steam 5 minutes or until salmon changes to pale pink. Remove plastic wrap. Sprinkle with bread crumbs; dot each with 1 Tbsp. butter. Place on broiler pan; broil 2 to 4 inches from heat until lightly browned.

Spoon about 3 Tbsp. sauce onto individual serving plates; place salmon on sauce. Garnish with fleurons and fried celery leaves.

*See Chef's Notes

BLACKENED PORK CHOPS

A refreshing pineapple-mint chutney contrasts the spicy blackened pork. This delightful Cajun dish is to be enjoyed with another southern favorite – corn fritters.

PINEAPPLE-MINT CHUTNEY

1 cup	fresh pineapple chunks
3 Tbsp.	sugar
2 Tbsp.	white vinegar
2 Tbsp.	lemon juice
2 Tbsp.	mint jelly
2 Tbsp.	chopped fresh mint
6	(8 oz. each) center cut pork chops
½ cup	Cajun spices*

CORN FRITTERS

1 cup	corn
2 Tbsp.	all-purpose flour
1	egg
2 Tbsp.	cold water
	Pinch baking powder

Grill or broil pineapple until evenly browned; chop into small cubes. In small saucepan heat sugar over medium heat until melted and golden. When sugar is melted stir in vinegar, lemon juice and mint jelly. Simmer briefly; stir in pineapple. Remove from heat; stir in mint. Cool.

Sprinkle both sides of pork chops with spices. Place on broiler pan. Broil 4 to 6 inches from heat 10 to 14 minutes, turning once. Reduce heat to 350 degrees. Continue cooking in oven until desired doneness.

Cream or mash ½ cup corn. In medium bowl stir together creamed corn, corn and remaining ingredients; stir until well mixed. Season to taste with salt and pepper. Using small ice cream scoop or teaspoon, scoop batter onto hot griddle or frying pan to form ½-inch rounds. Cook until golden on both sides, turning once.

Place pork chop on serving dish. Spoon 2 Tbsp. pineapple-mint chutney over each chop. Serve with corn fritters and peas with mushrooms.

*See Chef's Notes

ZUCCHINI AND EGGPLANT PARMIGIANA

Two meaty vegetables are the primary ingredients of this traditional meatless meal. Vegetarian or not, it's one to be enjoyed over and over again.

1 cup	all-purpose flour
2 lb.	zucchini, sliced lengthwise
1 lb.	eggplant, sliced lengthwise
	Vegetable oil
1½ cups	basic tomato sauce*
1 cup	shredded mozzarella cheese

Heat oven to 400 degrees. In shallow dish combine flour with salt and pepper to taste. Dip zucchini and eggplant into flour mixture. In large frying pan heat oil until hot over medium-high heat. Add zucchini and eggplant in one layer; cook until lightly browned and fork tender. Remove cooked vegetables; repeat with remaining vegetables. Arrange in individual (2-cup) casseroles in the following order: zucchini, eggplant, tomato sauce and cheese. Repeat, ending with cheese. Bake 10 to 15 minutes or until heated through and cheese is melted.

*See Chef's Notes

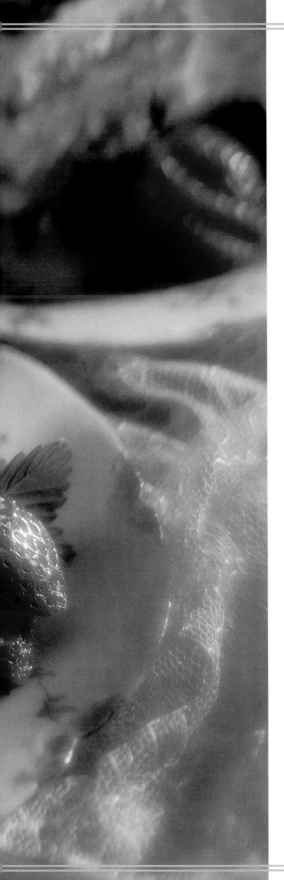

DESSERTS

What follows is an opulent spectrum of enticing desserts meant to punctuate the end of an extremely delectable meal. The variety of tastes is abounding. Each one has a certain flair for grandeur. All of them accomplish their purpose unequivocally.

Tiramisù, p.102

TIRAMISÙ

SERVES 6

A layered dessert that combines Kahlua and Grand Marnier with sponge cake and ladyfingers. What a splendid creation.

½	recipe vanilla sponge cake*
1 cup	hot water
½ cup	sugar
1 Tbsp.	espresso powder
2 Tbsp.	Kahlua or coffee-flavored liqueur
24	ladyfingers
2	egg yolks
¼ cup	sugar
2 cups	mascarpone cheese
1¼ cups	whipping cream, whipped
¼ cup	Grand Marnier or orange-flavored liqueur
1	recipe creme anglaise*
¼ cup	Kahlua or coffee-flavored liqueur
	Semi-sweet chocolate flakes
6	strawberry fans

Heat oven to 350 degrees. Refer to vanilla sponge cake recipe in Chef's Notes. Grease and flour a 6×8-inch baking pan. Prepare ½ recipe vanilla sponge cake; pour batter into prepared pan. Bake 15 minutes or until wooden pick inserted in center comes out clean. Cool 5 minutes; remove from pan. Cool completely on wire rack.

In small bowl combine water, sugar and espresso; stir until sugar and espresso are dissolved. Stir in Kahlua; cool. Place sponge cake and ladyfingers on wire rack; brush generously with syrup.

Line 6×8-inch pan with parchment paper. In small bowl combine egg yolks and sugar; mix well. Add mascarpone cheese; stir with rubber spatula until well mixed. Fold whipped cream and Grand Marnier into mascarpone mixture. Spoon layer ½ inch thick in bottom of prepared pan.

Place 8 soaked ladyfingers over mascarpone mixture. Repeat 2 times with remaining mascarpone mixture and ladyfingers. Fit soaked sponge cake over top for final layer. Cover; refrigerate 4 hours.

Prepare creme anglaise as directed; stir in Kahlua. Chill. Unmold tiramisu; cut into 6 portions. Sprinkle top with chocolate flakes. Serve with Kahlua sauce and strawberry fan.

*See Chef's Notes

Tips: If 6×8-inch pan is unavailable a 5×9-inch pan can be used. Some adjustments will need to be made to recipe.

Because of food safety, only pasteurized eggs should be used in recipes where the eggs are not cooked.

CAPPUCCINO PIE

SERVES 8

This coffee-flavored pie is made even more special with whipped cream rosettes and a crescent of chocolate.

2 oz.	semi-sweet chocolate
1 quart	mocha ice cream, softened
1	(9-inch) graham cracker pie shell
1½ cups	whipping cream, whipped
¼ cup	chocolate syrup

In small saucepan melt chocolate over low heat; pour onto waxed paper. Refrigerate until set; cut 8 half moon crescents for garnish. Spread softened ice cream into pie shell; smooth top with spatula. Freeze until firm. Reserve about 2 Tbsp. whipped cream for piping rosettes on pie. Spread remaining whipped cream over ice cream; freeze. Cut pie into 8 slices. On dessert plates spoon 1 to 2 tsp. chocolate syrup; place pie in syrup. Pipe whipped cream rosette on each slice; garnish with chocolate crescents.

FRUIT TRANCHE

SERVES 6

*W*hat an exceptional way to enjoy a serving of fruit. Serve it chilled with kiwi sauce.

10 oz.	puff pastry dough
¼ cup	whipping cream, whipped
1	recipe vanilla pastry cream*, chilled
6	slices pineapple, cut in half
6	slices peaches
3	strawberries, quartered
1	kiwi fruit, peeled, sliced
6	seedless red grapes
¼ cup	strained apricot preserves

KIWI SAUCE

¼ cup	sugar
2 Tbsp.	water
1	kiwi fruit, peeled

*H*eat oven to 425 degrees. On lightly floured board roll pastry into 5×14-inch rectangle. Pastry should be about ¼ inch thick. Cut 2 (½-inch) strips off long edge of dough. Place on baking sheet; lay strips along both sides and press lightly. Prick with a fork; brush with water. Place baking sheet on top to prevent sides from falling off. Bake for 30 minutes or until golden brown. Cool completely.

In large bowl fold whipped cream into pastry cream. Pipe mixture onto baked pastry. Mark into 6 portions. Arrange 1 slice pineapple, 1 slice peach, 1 slice pineapple, 2 quarters strawberries, kiwi slice and red grape on each. Brush with apricot glaze. Cut into 6 portions.

In small saucepan combine sugar and water. Bring to a full rolling boil over high heat; remove from heat. Cool completely. In blender container combine kiwi and syrup; blend until smooth. Serve Fruit Tranche with kiwi sauce. Store in refrigerator.

*See Chef's Notes

APPLE PIE

SERVES 8

Here's an extremely simple way to assemble an apple pie. Of course, no one needs to know how easy it was.

18 oz.	canned sliced apples
1¼ cups	sugar
1 tsp.	cinnamon
1	(9-inch) frozen pie shell
¼ cup	margarine, softened
1¼ cups	all-purpose flour
⅛ tsp.	salt
½ cup	shortening
3 Tbsp.	ice water
1	egg
1 Tbsp.	margarine, melted
	Whipped cream

Heat oven to 400 degrees. In large bowl combine apples, sugar and cinnamon; toss gently. Spoon into pie shell; dot with margarine. Set aside. In medium bowl mix flour and salt; cut in shortening until mixture resembles coarse crumbs. Add ice water; mix until mixture forms a dough. On lightly floured board roll out dough to 10-inch circle. Place dough over filled pie shell; crimp edges to seal. Cut slits in several places in pastry top. In small bowl beat egg and melted margarine until well mixed; brush over crust. Bake 50 to 60 minutes or until golden brown. Cool. Cut pie into 8 slices. Pipe whipped cream rosette on each slice.

CHOCOLATE DECADENCE

SERVES 16

As the name implies, this is a wickedly wonderful chocolate dessert that's impossible to resist.

1 lb.	semi-sweet chocolate, chopped
2 Tbsp.	whipping cream
6 Tbsp.	butter, softened
¼ cup	Myers rum
6	egg yolks
½ cup	sugar
1½ cups	whipping cream
1	recipe chocolate sponge cake*
1 cup	chocolate ganache*
	Whipped cream
	Mint leaves
	Strawberry sauce*

In medium saucepan melt semi-sweet chocolate over low heat; stir in whipping cream. Cool. When cool enough that butter will not melt, beat in butter. Stir in rum. In large bowl beat egg yolks and sugar on high speed for 5 minutes or until very light; fold into chocolate mixture. In large bowl beat whipping cream until soft peaks form; fold into chocolate mixture. Pour into parchment-lined 8-inch round baking pan. Cut chocolate sponge cake into ¼ inch thick slices; fit onto top of chocolate decadence. Refrigerate overnight. Remove from pan, placing cake layer on bottom. Spread top with ¾ cup chocolate ganache; refrigerate at least 10 minutes. Cut into 16 slices; pipe whipped cream rosette on each slice. Drizzle strawberry sauce on serving plate. Garnish with mint leaf. Store in refrigerator.

See Chef's Notes

Tip: Because of food safety, only pasteurized eggs should be used in recipes where the eggs are not cooked.

CRÊPES SUZETTE

SERVES 6

While there are several accounts as to the origin of this treat, there is but one way to describe it – excellent!

ORANGE SAUCE

1¼ cups sugar
¾ cup freshly squeezed orange juice
1 Tbsp. butter, melted
⅛ tsp. grated orange rind
1 Tbsp. Grand Marnier or orange-flavored liqueur

CRÊPES

4 Tbsp. sifted cake flour
3½ Tbsp. sifted bread flour
2 Tbsp. sugar
⅛ tsp. salt
1 egg
1 egg yolk
½ cup warm milk
2 Tbsp. butter, melted
2 tsp. brandy

Melted butter

*I*n small saucepan cook sugar over medium heat until melted and golden, stirring constantly. Stir in orange juice; mix until well blended. Stir in butter and orange rind; boil 1 to 1½ minutes or until slightly thickened. Stir in Grand Marnier. Keep warm.

Sift together cake flour, bread flour, sugar and salt; set aside. In medium bowl whisk egg and egg yolk until well blended. Stir in milk, butter and brandy; whisk until well blended. Slowly whisk in flour mixture until smooth. Do not whisk too much or batter will be bubbly and crêpes may have holes. Heat 5-inch nonstick crêpe pan over high heat 2 minutes; reduce heat to medium. Brush pan with melted butter; spoon 1½ Tbsp. batter into pan. Tilt pan so batter covers bottom of pan. Cook crêpe until light brown on both sides, turning once. Keep warm.

Fold crêpes into triangles; place 2 on each serving plate. Spoon 3 to 4 Tbsp. hot orange sauce over crêpes.

MENU

FIESTA

It's hot, exciting, and you can almost feel the samba beat. Tonight we celebrate the spirit of Carnivale with festive cuisine and all the color of a fiesta.

∿∿∿

FRIED CALAMARI WITH SALSA PICANTE
TEQUILA LIME SHRIMP

∿∿∿

BLACK BEAN SOUP
CHILLED CUCUMBER SOUP

∿∿∿

PASTA WITH SUN-DRIED TOMATOES AND SMOKED TURKEY
GRILLED NEW ZEALAND LAMB CHOPS
JERK CORNISH HEN
CHURRASCO

∿∿∿

CHILLED KEY LIME PIE
CHOCOLATE TRES LECHE

CHILLED KEY LIME PIE

SERVES 8

A luscious recipe that's famous in Florida. This simple version makes preparation a breeze.

1	(9-inch) graham cracker pie shell
1½ cups	sweetened condensed milk
¾ cup	lime juice
1	egg yolk
¼ tsp.	grated lime rind
6 Tbsp.	whipping cream, whipped
⅛ tsp.	green food color
1¾ tsp.	unflavored gelatin
1 Tbsp.	water
1 cup	whipping cream
2 Tbsp.	powdered sugar
8	lime slices

Heat oven to 350 degrees. Bake graham cracker pie shell 4 to 5 minutes or until lightly browned. Cool.

In medium bowl combine condensed milk, lime juice, egg yolk and rind; whisk until well mixed. Set aside. Fold whipped cream into condensed milk mixture; fold in food color. In small saucepan sprinkle gelatin over 1 Tbsp. water to soften; cook over low heat until completely dissolved. Cool slightly. Fold into filling. Pour into pie shell. Refrigerate 2 to 3 hours or until chilled.

In medium bowl beat whipping cream and powdered sugar on high speed until stiff. Remove about 2 Tbsp. Spread remaining whipped cream over pie filling. Cut pie into 8 slices. Pipe whipped cream rosette on each slice; garnish with lime slice. Store in refrigerator.

Tip: Because of food safety, only pasteurized eggs should be used in recipes where the eggs are not cooked.

Irish Cream Mousse Torte

SERVES 5

*I*rish Cream liqueur adds a special flavor to both the layer cake and the mousse. A whipped cream frosting is the crowning touch.

½	recipe chocolate sponge cake*
¼ cup	sugar
½ cup	hot water
1½ Tbsp.	Carolans Irish Cream Liqueur

MOUSSE

4 oz.	white chocolate, melted
3 Tbsp.	hot milk
1 Tbsp.	Carolans Irish Cream Liqueur
1 cup	whipping cream, whipped
1	egg white
1 Tbsp.	sugar
¾ tsp.	unflavored gelatin
1 Tbsp.	water

¾ cup	whipping cream
4 tsp.	powdered sugar

Walnut halves
Chocolate sauce*

Heat oven to 350 degrees. Refer to chocolate sponge cake in Chef's Notes. Prepare half of recipe reducing all ingredients. Bake in 6-inch round baking pan. Baking time will be reduced. Remove from pan; cool completely. Slice into 2 thin layers. In small bowl combine sugar and water; stir until sugar is dissolved. Stir in liqueur. Brush both layers generously with syrup. Place 1 layer in parchment-lined 6-inch round baking pan. Set aside.

Place warm melted white chocolate in medium bowl; stir in hot milk. Stir until smooth; add liqueur. Cool completely. Fold whipped cream into white chocolate mixture until just mixed. In small bowl beat egg white and sugar until soft peaks form; fold into mousse. In small saucepan sprinkle gelatin over water; cook over low heat until dissolved. Cool slightly. Fold into mousse; do not over mix. Spoon mousse into cake pan; cover with reserved cake layer. Refrigerate 3 hours or until set.

In medium bowl beat whipping cream and powdered sugar until stiff. Remove about 2 Tbsp. Carefully unmold cake. Place on cake plate. Frost top and sides with whipped cream. Cut into 5 servings. Pipe whipped cream rosette on each slice; garnish with walnut half. Serve with hot or cold chocolate sauce. Store in refrigerator.

*See Chef's Notes

Tip: Because of food safety, only pasteurized eggs should be used in recipes where the eggs are not cooked.

COCONUT MOUSSE TORTE

SERVES 6

*C*oconut and pineapple – two gifts from the
tropics. They are both thoroughly enjoyed in
this light, fluffy torte.

½ recipe vanilla sponge cake*

COCONUT MOUSSE FILLING

4	egg yolks
3 Tbsp.	sugar
¼ cup	cream of coconut
2 tsp.	coconut extract
¾ cup	whipping cream
¾ tsp.	unflavored gelatin
3 Tbsp.	water
½ cup	whipping cream
1 Tbsp.	powdered sugar
½ cup	shredded coconut, toasted
6	strawberries or maraschino cherries
	Pineapple sauce*

*H*eat oven to 350 degrees. Refer to vanilla
sponge cake recipe in Chef's Notes.
Prepare half of recipe reducing all ingredients. Bake in greased and floured 6-inch
round baking pan. Baking time will be reduced. Remove from pan; cool completely. Slice into 2 thin layers; place
1 layer in parchment-lined 6-inch round
baking pan. Reserve remaining layer.

In small bowl combine egg yolks and
sugar; whisk until light and fluffy. Add
cream of coconut and coconut extract; stir
until well mixed. In medium bowl beat
whipping cream on high speed until stiff.
Fold into coconut mixture until just
mixed. In small saucepan sprinkle gelatin
over water; cook over low heat until dissolved. Cool slightly. Fold into mousse;
do not over mix. Spoon mousse into cake
pan; cover with reserved cake layer.
Refrigerate 3 hours or until set.

In medium bowl beat whipping cream
and powdered sugar until stiff. Remove
about 2 Tbsp. Carefully unmold cake.
Place on cake plate. Frost top and sides
with whipped cream. Press toasted coconut on sides. Cut into 5 slices. Pipe
whipped cream rosette on each slice; garnish with strawberry. Serve with pineapple
sauce. Store in refrigerator.

*See Chef's Notes

*Tip: Because of food safety, only pasteurized eggs
should be used in recipes where the eggs are not
cooked.*

BLUEBERRY COBBLER

SERVES 12

A delicious streusel recipe that's a blueberry lover's delight. Top with vanilla ice cream.

2½ lb.	frozen blueberries
1⅓ cups	sugar
¼ cup	cornstarch
¼ cup	water

STREUSEL

2¼ cups	cake flour
1½ cups	powdered sugar
⅔ cup	margarine
½ tsp.	vanilla
¼ tsp.	cinnamon

12	scoops vanilla ice cream
	Whipped cream
12	toasted almond slices

Heat oven to 350 degrees. Place blueberries and sugar in large saucepan. Bring to a boil over medium-high heat, stirring constantly. Reduce heat to low; cook 20 minutes. In small bowl mix cornstarch and water. Pour into blueberries; stir constantly until thickened. Cook an additional 2 to 3 minutes. Set aside. In medium bowl combine streusel ingredients on low speed; mix until crumbly. Pour blueberries into 9×13-inch baking dish; sprinkle with streusel. Bake 20 to 30 minutes or until golden brown and bubbly. Cool.

Scoop cobbler into dessert dishes. Top with scoop of ice cream. Pipe whipped cream rosette on cobbler; garnish with toasted almond.

BANANA FLAMBÉ

SERVES 12

There is nothing that impresses guests more than a flaming dessert. But this one happens to be more than showy. It's positively delectable.

8	bananas, peeled, sliced ⅜-inch thick
1 Tbsp.	lemon juice
⅛ tsp.	cinnamon
⅛ tsp.	grated nutmeg

ORANGE SAUCE

1½ cups	water
6 Tbsp.	frozen orange juice concentrate
1 Tbsp.	grated orange rind
⅛ tsp.	salt
	Orange food color
3 Tbsp.	cornstarch
½ cup	water
2 Tbsp.	Grand Marnier or orange-flavored liqueur
2 Tbsp.	banana liqueur

TUTTI FRUTTI, IF DESIRED

12	scoops vanilla ice cream
6 Tbsp.	151 proof white rum

In medium bowl mix bananas with lemon juice, cinnamon and nutmeg; set aside.

In medium saucepan combine 1 cup water, orange juice concentrate, orange rind, salt and food coloring. Bring to a boil over medium heat. Reduce heat to low; simmer 5 minutes. In small bowl combine cornstarch and ½ cup water; mix well. Add to juice mixture, stirring constantly. Continue cooking, stirring constantly, until mixture is thickened and clear. Gently mix bananas, Grand Marnier and banana liqueur into sauce. Place scoop of ice cream in each serving dish. Spoon warm bananas over ice cream. Top each with Tutti Frutti, if desired. Place about 2 tsp. rum in flambé cup or metal ladle. Carefully ignite rum; pour over each dessert. Serve.

Tip: Red and yellow food colors can be used to make orange.

CHOCOLATE CAKE

A *three-layer chocolate cake makes a grand impression. Serve this one with strawberry sauce and cherries for an unforgettable experience.*

1	recipe devil's food sponge cake*
⅓ cup	sugar
½ cup	hot water
1 Tbsp.	Myers rum
2	recipes chocolate buttercream*
	Chocolate ganache*
8	cherries with stems
	Strawberry sauce*

*P*repare cake as directed in Chef's Notes. Cool completely; slice into 3 layers. In small bowl mix sugar, water and rum; stir until sugar is dissolves. Brush generously onto cake layers. Reserve about ¼ cup buttercream for garnish. Spread remaining chocolate buttercream between layers and on top of cake. Refrigerate 10 minutes. Pour ganache over top; refrigerate 10 minutes. Cut into 2×4-inch slices. Pipe rosette onto each; garnish with cherry. Serve with strawberry sauce. Store in refrigerator.

*See Chef's Notes

BAKED STUFFED APPLES

*N*ow these are tempting apples. It's a time-tested recipe that continues to satisfy.

10	apples
½ cup	raisins
½ cup	slivered almonds
½ tsp.	cinnamon
½ tsp.	grated nutmeg
2¼ cups	water
1	(6 oz.) can frozen orange juice concentrate, thawed
3 Tbsp.	honey

*H*eat oven to 375 degrees. Remove core from apples; do not remove bottom. Place in baking dish. In small bowl combine raisins, almonds, cinnamon and nutmeg. Divide filling among apples. In small bowl combine water, orange juice concentrate and honey; mix until well blended. Pour over apples. Bake for 50 minutes or until apples are tender. Place in dessert dishes; spoon cooking juices over top.

Tip: Use Granny Smith, Golden Delicious or other cooking apples for this recipe.

CHOCOLATE
PIECE DE RESISTANCE

SERVES 6

*T*he name says it all. This is the dessert to end
all desserts.

FILLING

6 oz.	semi-sweet chocolate, chopped
1 Tbsp.	hot whipping cream
2 Tbsp.	Myers rum
5 Tbsp.	sugar, divided
3	egg yolks
1	egg white
1¼ tsp.	unflavored gelatin
2 Tbsp.	water
6	(5×8½-inch) pieces parchment paper
6 oz.	semi-sweet chocolate, chopped

Strawberry sauce*
Strawberries
Peach slices
Mint leaves

*I*n small saucepan melt chocolate over low
heat; remove from heat. Stir in whipping
cream; mix well. Stir in rum. In small
bowl whisk 3 Tbsp. sugar and egg yolks
until very light; fold into chocolate mixture. In small bowl beat egg white on high
speed until soft peaks form; gradually beat
in 2 Tbsp. sugar. Fold into chocolate mixture. In small saucepan sprinkle gelatin
over water; cook over low heat until dissolved. Cool slightly. Fold into chocolate
mixture. Refrigerate at least 1 hour. Do
not pipe mixture until it is set.

Roll paper into cylinder 2¼ inches across
the top and 1¼ inches across the bottom;
secure with tape on inside. Trim top to
form even edge. Place juice glass or ice
cream cone inside to hold shape. Melt
chocolate over boiling water until it is
105 degrees, stirring constantly. Do not

allow chocolate to reach higher temperature. Place in plastic bag; cut off corner so
thin layer of chocolate can be piped. Pipe
chocolate around paper cone leaving
about ⅛ inch between strips. When dry,
repeat piping process, piping up and
down forming cone with open spaces. Set
aside to set completely. Carefully loosen
paper and lift out. With remaining chocolate pipe base 2¼ inches square, using
zigzag strips. When dry; repeat 2 times.
Set aside to dry completely. Secure cone
to base with melted chocolate. Pipe set
chocolate filling into cone, allowing some
to come out slightly from holes in the
cone. Serve with strawberry sauce.
Garnish with strawberries, peaches and
mint leaves.

See Chef's Notes

*Tip: Because of food safety, only pasteurized eggs
should be used in recipes where the eggs are not
cooked.*

CHOCOLATE ECLAIR

SERVES 12

The best bakery secret is out. But these eclairs are better than bakery-made. Serve them fresh and garnish with pistachios.

1½ cups	water
½ cup	margarine
1 tsp.	sugar
⅛ tsp.	salt
2¼ cups	all-purpose flour
9	eggs
¼ cup	whipping cream, whipped
2	recipes chocolate pastry cream, chilled*
14 oz.	semi-sweet chocolate, chopped
1 Tbsp.	butter, melted
¾ cup	hot milk
½ cup	hot whipping cream
	Whipped cream
12	pistachios

Heat oven to 425 degrees. In medium saucepan combine water, margarine, sugar and salt; bring to a boil over medium heat. Stir flour into boiling mixture; continue cooking 3 minutes, stirring constantly. Remove from heat. Place in large bowl; beat in eggs, one at a time, until well mixed. Beat mixture 3 minutes on medium. Form eclairs by piping choux paste 4-inches long, 1½-inches wide and 1-inch thick onto baking sheet. Bake 30 minutes until golden brown. Cool completely on wire racks.

In large bowl fold whipped cream into chilled chocolate pastry cream. Pipe filling into eclairs.

Melt semi-sweet chocolate over low heat; stir in butter. Stir in hot milk and hot cream; stir until smooth. Spread chocolate on top of eclair. Refrigerate at least 10 minutes. Pipe each with whipped cream rosette; garnish with pistachio.

NAPOLEON

SERVES 16

It's hard to say what's more famous – Napoleon, the Frenchman, or this dessert. One thing's for certain, this one will go down in history with guests.

1 lb.	puff pastry dough
2	recipes vanilla pastry cream, chilled*
¼ cup	whipping cream, whipped
Approx. 1 cup	fondant*
¼ cup	semi-sweet chocolate chips, melted
	Strawberry sauce*

Heat oven to 375 degrees. On lightly floured board roll out puff pastry to 17×24-inch rectangle. Let rest 30 minutes. Cut into 4 (8½×12-inch) sheets. Place on parchment-lined baking sheets; prick with a fork. Bake 25 minutes or until golden brown. Cool completely on wire rack. Cut each into 12 (2½×3-inch) pieces. (There will be 48 pieces.)

In large bowl fold whipped cream into vanilla pastry cream. For each dessert use 3 pieces of pastry. Pipe pastry cream mixture between layers. For top layer, heat fondant in double boiler to 110 degrees. Pour over tops of Napoleons. Pipe thin lines of melted chocolate over fondant; pull wooden pick through chocolate for decoration. Store in refrigerator. Serve with strawberry sauce.

See Chef's Notes

KAHLUA CHEESECAKE

SERVES 16

*A*nother fabulous way to enjoy coffee after dinner. Serving it with brewed coffee would not be redundant.

3	(8-oz.) pkg. cream cheese, softened
¾ cup	sugar
¾ cup	sour cream
7 Tbsp.	cornstarch
1 Tbsp.	vanilla
4	eggs
1 cup	milk
¼ cup	Kahlua or coffee-flavored liqueur

KAHLUA SAUCE

1	recipe creme anglaise*
¼ cup	Kahlua or coffee-flavored liqueur
½ cup	toasted sliced almonds

*H*eat oven to 325 degrees. In large mixer bowl beat cream cheese on medium speed until smooth and creamy, scraping sides of bowl often. Add sugar and sour cream; beat until smooth and well blended. Beat in cornstarch and vanilla; mix well. Beat in eggs, one at a time; continue beating until smooth and creamy. On low speed beat in milk and Kahlua. Pour into lightly greased 9-inch Springform pan. Place shallow pan half full of water on lower oven rack. Place cheesecake on middle oven rack. Bake 1 hour or until set. Cool in pan on wire rack. Refrigerate 4 hours or overnight before serving.

Prepare creme anglaise as directed; stir in Kahlua. Chill. Slice cheesecake into 16 slices. Spoon 1 Tbsp. Kahlua sauce over each; sprinkle with toasted sliced almonds.

*See Chef's Notes

BANANA CREAM PIE

SERVES 8

*A*nyone can make homemade pie with this favorite. Top it with real whipped cream and banana slices.

1	(9-inch) graham cracker pie shell
1	large banana, sliced
¼ cup	+ 3 Tbsp. sugar
2 cups	milk, divided
5½ Tbsp.	cornstarch
2	egg yolks
1 tsp.	vanilla
1 tsp.	banana extract
¾ cup	whipping cream
1 Tbsp.	powdered sugar
8	banana slices
	Pineapple or orange sauce*

*H*eat oven to 350 degrees. Bake graham cracker pie shell 4 to 5 minutes or until lightly browned. Cool. Arrange sliced bananas on bottom of shell.

In medium saucepan heat sugar and 1¼ cups milk until mixture just comes to a boil over medium-high heat. In small bowl combine remaining milk, cornstarch, egg yolks, vanilla and banana extract. Stir a small amount of hot milk into yolk mixture to warm. Gradually whisk warmed yolk mixture into hot milk. Continue cooking, stirring constantly, until mixture comes to a full boil. Pour hot pudding into pie shell. Smooth surface with spatula. Refrigerate until set.

In medium bowl beat whipping cream and powdered sugar on high speed until stiff. Remove about 2 Tbsp. Spread remaining whipped cream over pie filling. Cut pie into 8 slices. Pipe whipped cream rosette on each slice; garnish with banana slice. Serve with pineapple or orange sauce.

*See Chef's Notes

Tip: Brush banana slices with lemon juice to prevent darkening.

GUAVA CREAM CHEESE NAPOLEON

SERVES 5

*T*his French pastry is prepared with a variety of fillings. Guava lends this one a sweet, fruity taste.

1½ lb.	puff pastry dough
1	egg, beaten
⅓ cup	sugar
1½ cups	guava paste
1	(8-oz.) pkg. cream cheese, softened
1	recipe vanilla pastry cream*
4 Tbsp.	powdered sugar
	Mint leaves
1	recipe creme anglaise*

*H*eat oven to 375 degrees. On lightly floured board roll puff pastry to rectangle 9½ × 15½-inches. Pastry should be about ¹⁄₁₆-inch thick. Pierce with a fork; let rest 15 to 20 minutes. Cut into 15 (3 inch) squares. Place on baking sheet. Brush with egg wash and sprinkle with sugar. Bake for 15 to 18 minutes or until golden brown. Cool completely on wire rack.

Place guava paste in small metal bowl; place over hot water to melt paste. Place cream cheese in medium bowl; beat until smooth. Gradually stir in melted guava paste; beat until smooth. Prepare pastry cream; cool to 110 degrees. Gradually stir in cream cheese mixture; stir until smooth. Chill. For each dessert use 3 squares pastry; pipe filling between layers. Sprinkle top with powdered sugar; garnish with mint. Serve each with 3 to 4 Tbsp. creme anglaise.

*See Chef's Notes

CHOCOLATE FUDGE CAKE

SERVES 8

*A*s if this cake wasn't grandiose enough. It features melted chocolate piping in a diamond pattern for the top and sweet buttercream stars.

1	recipe devil's food sponge cake*

CHOCOLATE FUDGE FILLING

3⅓ cups	sugar
1½ cups	milk
¾ cup	water
1 tsp.	baking soda
7 oz.	semi-sweet chocolate, chopped
1 cup	butter, cut up
2 oz.	semi-sweet chocolate, melted
2	recipes chocolate buttercream*
	Chocolate sprinkles

*P*repare cake as directed in Chef's Notes. Cool completely. Slice into 2 layers.

In medium saucepan bring sugar, milk, water and baking soda to a boil over medium heat. Add chocolate and butter. Cook, stirring constantly, until mixture reaches 250 degrees on candy thermometer. Place 1 cake layer on serving plate. Spread with fudge filling; top with second layer. Spread remaining fudge filling on sides and top of cake. Let cool. Pipe melted chocolate on top of cake in straight parallel lines. Repeat, piping in opposite direction, forming diamond pattern. Cut into 2×4-inch slices. Using star tip pipe buttercream on sides of cake. Pipe rosettes on each slice; garnish with chocolate sprinkles.

*See Chef's Notes

CHERRIES JUBILEE

SERVES 14

Flaming sweet, red cherries over vanilla ice cream — it's cause for a jubilee.

1	(16-oz.) can dark sweet cherries
½ cup	sugar
2 Tbsp.	cornstarch
1 tsp.	cinnamon
2 tsp.	orange extract
½ tsp.	red food color
14	scoops vanilla ice cream
½ cup	151 proof white rum

Drain juice from cherries; reserve juice. In small saucepan combine juice, sugar, cornstarch, cinnamon, extract and food color; stir until well mixed. Cook over medium heat, stirring constantly, until mixture comes to a boil. Continue cooking, stirring constantly, until mixture is thickened and clear. Carefully stir in cherries. Place scoop of ice cream in each serving dish. Spoon warm cherries over ice cream. Place about 2 tsp. rum in flambé cup or metal ladle. Carefully ignite rum; pour over each dessert. Serve.

BANANA PUDDING

SERVES 10

There's never been a better banana pudding than this. Layers of vanilla wafers and strawberry topping take it beyond an ordinary dessert.

1 cup	sugar
2 cups	milk
2 tsp.	banana extract
2½ tsp.	cornstarch
¾ cup	milk
2	eggs, separated
2	egg whites
⅔ cup	sugar
3	bananas, sliced
4 oz.	vanilla wafers
½ cup	strawberry sauce*

In medium saucepan combine sugar, milk and extract. Bring to a boil over medium heat. Reduce heat to low. In small bowl combine cornstarch with ¾ cup milk; beat in egg yolks. Add about ½ cup hot milk to yolk mixture to warm. Stir yolk mixture into saucepan. Continue cooking, stirring constantly, until mixture thickens. Cook 1 minute. In medium bowl beat 4 egg whites on high speed until soft peaks form. Gradually add sugar; beat until stiff and glossy. Fold half into custard. Remaining half will be used as meringue on pudding.

Heat oven to 450 degrees. In 2-quart oven-proof dish layer custard, banana slices and vanilla wafers. Repeat layers until mixture is used up. Spread remaining meringue over dish, sealing to edges. Bake 5 minutes or until meringue is lightly browned. Refrigerate. Scoop pudding into dessert cup; pour 1 tsp. strawberry sauce over top.

See Chef's Notes

Tip: Because of food safety, only pasteurized eggs should be used in recipes where the eggs are not cooked.

PARIS BREST

SERVES 14

Nutty filled pastries garnished with chocolate ganache and cherries. Sensational.

1¾ cups	water
¾ cup	margarine
6 Tbsp.	butter
1 tsp.	sugar
¼ tsp.	salt
2¼ cups	all-purpose flour
10	eggs
¼ cup	sliced almonds
1 oz.	praline paste
2 Tbsp.	milk
2	recipes vanilla pastry cream*, chilled
¾ cup	whipping cream, whipped
	Powdered sugar
¼ cup	chocolate ganache*
14	maraschino cherries with stems

Heat oven to 400 degrees. In medium saucepan combine water, margarine, butter, sugar and salt; bring to a boil over medium heat. Stir flour into boiling mixture; continue cooking 3 minutes. Remove from heat. Place in large bowl; beat in eggs, one at a time, until well mixed. Beat mixture 3 minutes on medium. Form pastries by piping choux paste with star tip into 14 circles about 2¾ inches across and ¾ inch thick onto baking sheet. Center should remain open. Sprinkle with almonds. Bake 10 minutes until mixture starts puffing up; reduce heat to 375 degrees. Bake 25 minutes more or until golden brown. Cool completely on wire racks. Slice into two layers.

In small bowl mix praline paste with milk until well mixed; stir into pastry cream. Fold about ¾ cup whipped cream into pastry cream. Pipe praline cream onto bottoms of pastry; top each with a little of remaining whipped cream. Place top of Paris Brest over filling; sprinkle with powdered sugar. Garnish with chocolate ganache and cherry. Store in refrigerator.

*See Chef's Notes

CHOCOLATE TRES LECHE

SERVES 8

There are three captivating reasons why this dessert has become one of our most popular finales—chocolate, chocolate, chocolate!

¾ cup	sifted cake flour
2 Tbsp.	unsweetened cocoa
½ cup	sugar
4	eggs
2	egg yolks
1½ tsp.	vegetable oil
2 cups	evaporated milk
1¼ cups	sweetened condensed milk
1 cup	whipping cream
¼ cup	Kahlua or coffee-flavored liqueur
2 Tbsp.	chocolate syrup
¼ cup	powdered sugar
1 Tbsp.	unsweetened cocoa
1 cup	whipping cream
2½ Tbsp.	Kahlua or coffee-flavored liqueur

Heat oven to 375 degrees. Line bottom of 9-inch square baking pan with parchment paper. Sift together flour and cocoa; set aside. In large mixer bowl beat sugar, eggs and egg yolks on high speed until very light, about 5 minutes. Fold in flour mixture. Fold in oil. Pour into prepared pan. Bake 20 to 25 minutes or until cake springs back when touched lightly in center. Cool completely; remove from pan.

In medium bowl combine evaporated milk, condensed milk, cream, Kahlua and chocolate syrup; blend well. Place cake on 15×10×1-inch jelly-roll pan; spoon milk mixture over cake. Continue to spoon milk mixture over cake until cake is thoroughly soaked.

Sift powdered sugar and cocoa together; set aside. In medium bowl whip cream on high speed until soft peaks form. Gradually beat in powdered sugar mixture. Continue beating until stiff; fold in Kahlua. Using star tip, pipe onto top of cake. Cut cake into 8 portions (about 4×2 inches each). Store in refrigerator.

PASSION FRUIT INDULGENCE

SERVES 6

*O*f course this sponge cake is named for the fruit, but passion could also describe one's feeling for the dessert.

½	recipe vanilla sponge cake*
1 cup	passion fruit juice
5 tsp.	unflavored gelatin
½ cup	plain yogurt
1½ cups	Napoleon brandy
2 tsp.	passion fruit compound
1¼ cups	whipping cream, whipped
6 Tbsp.	sugar
3 Tbsp.	corn syrup
2 Tbsp.	water
2	egg whites
¼ tsp.	cream of tartar
½ cup	whipping cream
1½ tsp.	powdered sugar
	Strawberry sauce*

Heat oven to 350 degrees. Refer to vanilla sponge cake recipe in Chef's Notes. Grease and flour a 7-inch baking pan. Prepare ½ recipe Vanilla Sponge Cake, pour batter into prepared pan. Bake 15 minutes or until wooden pick inserted in center comes out clean. Cool 5 minutes, remove from pan. Cool completely on wire rack. Slice into 2 layers. Place 1 layer in parchment-lined 7-inch mold. Reserve remaining layer.

Place ½ cup passion fruit juice in small saucepan; sprinkle gelatin over juice to soften. Heat over low heat until gelatin is dissolved; cool slightly. In medium bowl stir together remaining juice, yogurt, brandy and passion fruit compound; mix well. Fold in whipped cream. Fold in gelatin.

In small saucepan combine sugar, corn syrup and water. Bring to a boil over medium heat; cook 1½ minutes. In medium bowl beat egg whites and cream of tartar on high until soft peaks form. While beating on high speed slowly pour hot syrup, drop by drop, into egg whites. Continue beating until stiff and glossy and cooled. Fold meringue into whipped cream mixture. Pour into mold, place remaining cake layer over filling. Chill until set.

Beat ½ cup whipping cream with powdered sugar until stiff. Carefully unmold dessert. Place on serving plate. Spread whipped cream on top and sides. Cut into 6 slices. Serve with strawberry sauce.

*See Chef's Notes

Tip: Because of food safety, only pasteurized eggs should be used in recipes where the eggs are not cooked.

WHITE CHOCO BREAD PUDDING

SERVES 5

There's something about white chocolate that takes desserts up a notch. This one is pure heaven.

4	slices white bread, crust removed, cubed
½ cup	whipping cream
2	egg yolks
3 Tbsp.	sugar
½ tsp.	vanilla
3 oz.	white chocolate, chopped
2 Tbsp.	butter, melted
2	egg whites
¼ tsp.	cream of tartar

Heat oven to 350 degrees. Grease 6-inch round mold with butter; sprinkle with sugar. Set aside. Soak bread in cream to soften. In small bowl whisk egg yolks, 2 Tbsp. sugar and vanilla until well blended. In small saucepan melt white chocolate over low heat; stir in melted butter. Cool slightly. Stir chocolate mixture into yolk mixture. In medium bowl beat egg whites, 1 Tbsp. sugar and cream of tartar until soft peaks form. Fold meringue into bread mixture; pour into prepared mold. Place mold in water bath; bake 35 to 40 minutes or until set in center. When baked, let cool slightly and unmold.

COCONUT CAKE

SERVES 16

Add home-made goodness to a simple white cake mix. Buttercream frosting, toasted coconut and vanilla wafers make it totally unique.

1	(18.25-oz.) box white cake mix
¾ tsp.	coconut extract

COCONUT FROSTING

2	recipes vanilla buttercream*
2 tsp.	coconut extract
10 oz.	toasted coconut
4 oz.	semi-sweet chocolate, melted
16	vanilla wafers

Heat oven to 350 degrees. Grease and flour 3 (9-inch) round baking pans. Prepare cake mix according to package directions adding ¾ tsp. coconut extract to batter. Pour batter into prepared pans. Bake according to package directions, reducing baking time. Cool 10 minutes; remove from pans. Cool completely on wire racks.

Prepare vanilla buttercream folding in 2 tsp. coconut extract. Remove about 2 Tbsp. to use as garnish. Place 1 cake layer on serving plate. Spread with buttercream; top with second layer. Repeat. Spread remaining buttercream on sides and top of cake. Coat sides with coconut. Drizzle melted chocolate on top of cake. Pipe 16 rosettes on top of cake; set vanilla wafer in each. Store in refrigerator.

See Chef's Notes

SWAN CHANTILLY

SERVES 12

A creative dessert that is as decorative as it is delicious. A delicate swan is crafted with a pastry tube, ice cream and a generous amount of imagination.

1½ cups	water
½ cup	margarine
2 Tbsp.	butter
1 tsp.	sugar
	Pinch salt
2½ cups	all-purpose flour
9	eggs
6 cups	pistachio ice cream
¼ cup	whipping cream, whipped
½ cup	chocolate syrup
¼ cup	pistachios

*H*eat oven to 425 degrees. In medium saucepan combine water, margarine, butter, sugar and salt; bring to a boil over medium heat. Stir flour into boiling mixture; continue cooking 3 minutes.

Remove from heat. Place in large bowl; beat in eggs, one at a time, until well mixed. Pipe 12 swan bodies (ovals) with star tip onto baking sheet. Place remaining choux paste in bag fitted with plain tip; pipe 12 swan necks onto separate baking sheet. Bake swan bodies 10 minutes until mixture starts puffing up; reduce heat to 375 degrees. Bake 20 minutes more or golden brown. Bake swan necks at 375 degrees 15 minutes. Cool completely on wire racks.

Cut about ⅓ off top of swan bodies; cut in half lengthwise to form swan wings. Place bodies on dessert plates; scoop ice cream into center. Pipe whipped cream toward front of body; attach neck so it leans back toward wings. Arrange wings on each side pointing upward. Pour about 1½ tsp. chocolate syrup to side of plate; sprinkle with pistachios.

Mango Custard Tart

Serves 8

*F*resh mango and Napoleon brandy make this custard a real taste treat. It's also a great guest pleaser.

½ cup	sugar
6 Tbsp.	milk
6 Tbsp.	whipping cream
¾ cup	mango puree
2	eggs, lightly beaten
4	egg yolks, lightly beaten
1½ Tbsp.	Napoleon brandy
1	(9-inch) frozen pie shell
¼ cup	whipping cream
1 Tbsp.	powdered sugar

*H*eat oven to 350 degrees. In small saucepan bring sugar, milk and whipping cream to a boil over medium heat. Remove from heat; cool slightly. Add mango puree, eggs, egg yolks and brandy. Whisk until well mixed and eggs are completely mixed in. Strain mixture into pie shell. Bake 30 to 35 minutes or until custard is set. Cool completely. Refrigerate until serving.

In small bowl beat whipping cream and powdered sugar until stiff. Cut pie into 8 slices. Pipe whipped cream rosette on each slice.

Tip: One ripe medium mango should yield about ¾ cup puree.

Baked Alaska

Serves 6

*T*he ice cream dessert that warms the heart. It makes a grand presentation offering three favorite flavors.

1	(18.25-oz.) box yellow cake mix
1 quart	Neapolitan ice cream
5	egg whites
¼ tsp.	cream of tartar
1¼ cups	sugar
6	cherries with stems

*P*repare cake as directed on package. Bake in 15×10×1-inch jelly-roll pan. Cool completely. Cut crosswise into 3 cakes. Reserve 2 cakes for another use. Slice remaining cake into 2 thin layers. Place 1 layer on cookie sheet. Cut ice cream into slices to fit cake. Place ice cream on bottom layer. Place remaining cake layer on ice cream; top with remaining ice cream. Freeze until firm, several hours or overnight.

Heat oven to 450 degrees. In large mixer bowl beat egg whites and cream of tartar on high speed until soft peaks form. Gradually beat in sugar, 1 Tbsp. at a time; continue beating until stiff peaks and sugar is dissolved. Remove base from freezer; spread with meringue. Carefully seal meringue to cookie sheet to prevent shrinkage. Bake 4 minutes or until lightly browned. Garnish with cherries. Serve immediately.

Tip: Can also be assembled and frozen in a large bowl.

POACHED PEARS

SERVES 6

*T*he simple preparation of poached pears will fill the air with a deliciously spicy aroma that prepares one's mouth for an exciting taste to come.

1 cup	sugar
¼ cup	red currant jelly
3	whole cloves
1	cinnamon stick
¼ tsp.	grated nutmeg
5 cups	water
1 cup	red wine
2 Tbsp.	lemon juice
6	fresh ripe pears

*P*lace all ingredients but pears in large saucepan; bring to a boil. Peel and core pears leaving stem intact. Add pears to liquid. Reduce heat to low; simmer pears until fork-tender. Chill pears in cooking liquid. Serve pears with chilled poaching liquid and frozen fat-free yogurt, if desired.

BLUEBERRY STATE OF MIND

SERVES 6

*B*lueberry season will be a welcome sight from now on. The taste is unprecedented.

3 cups	fresh blueberries
1½ cups	sugar
3 tsp.	cornstarch
3 Tbsp.	water
3	eggs, separated
½ cup	sugar, divided
⅓ cup	corn syrup
5 tsp.	brandy
3 tsp.	unflavored gelatin
3 Tbsp.	water
1½ cups	whipping cream, whipped
6	strawberry fans
	Mint leaves

*I*n medium saucepan combine blueberries and sugar. Bring to a boil over high heat; reduce heat to low. Cook about 20 minutes, stirring occasionally, until blueberries are cooked. In small bowl combine cornstarch and water; stir into blueberries. Continue cooking, stirring constantly, until thickened. Divide mixture in half; cool completely. Half of mixture will be used as sauce for dessert.

In medium bowl whisk egg yolks and 6 Tbsp. sugar until light and fluffy. Stir in corn syrup and brandy; fold into blueberry mixture. In small saucepan sprinkle gelatin over water; cook over low heat until dissolved. Stir into blueberry mixture. Fold whipped cream into blueberry mixture. In medium bowl beat egg whites on high speed until soft peaks form. Add remaining 2 Tbsp. sugar; continue beating until sugar is dissolved. Fold into blueberry mixture. Pipe mixture into 6 or 7 (5 oz.) ramekins. Refrigerate at least 3 hours.

Unmold dessert from ramekins by dipping in hot water. Spoon 2 Tbsp. reserved blueberry sauce over each. Place strawberry fans and mint leaves on each plate.

Tip: Because of food safety, only pasteurized eggs should be used in recipes where the eggs are not cooked.

CHEESECAKE

This cheesecake stands alone. The strawberry sauce, however, stands on tradition.

	3	(8-oz.) pkg. cream cheese, softened
3/4 cup	sugar
3/4 cup	sour cream
1/4 cup	cornstarch
1 1/4 tsp.	lemon juice
1 Tbsp.	vanilla
3	eggs
3/4 cup	milk
1/4 cup	whipping cream, whipped
16	strawberry slices
	Strawberry sauce*

Heat oven to 325 degrees. In large mixer bowl beat cream cheese on medium speed until smooth and creamy, scraping sides of bowl often. Add sugar and sour cream; beat until smooth and well blended. Beat in cornstarch, lemon juice and vanilla; mix well. Beat in eggs, one at a time; continue beating until smooth and creamy. On low speed beat in milk. Pour into lightly greased 9-inch Springform pan. Place shallow pan half full of water on lower oven rack. Place cheesecake on middle oven rack. Bake 1 hour or until set. Cool in pan on wire rack. Refrigerate 4 hours or overnight before serving.

Cut cheesecake into 8 slices. Pipe whipped cream rosette on each slice; garnish with strawberry. Serve with strawberry sauce.

See Chef's Notes

BLACK FOREST

The Germans are known for their baking expertise. This recipe originated in the Black Forest region. One taste and there's no question how it became so famous.

1	recipe devil's food sponge cake*
1	(15-oz.) can sweet dark cherries
6 Tbsp.	sugar
1/4 cup	Kirschwasser
1 3/4 tsp	unflavored gelatin
2 Tbsp.	water
2 cups	whipping cream
2 1/2 Tbsp.	powdered sugar
1	(8 oz.) bar semi-sweet chocolate

Prepare cake as directed in Chef's Notes. Cool completely; slice into 3 layers.

Drain cherries, reserving juice. In medium bowl combine juice, sugar and Kirschwasser; stir until sugar is dissolved. Stir in cherries; marinate 20 minutes. Remove cherries from juice; let drain. Set aside 8 cherries for garnish. Brush cherry juice mixture generously on cake layers. In small saucepan sprinkle gelatin over water; cook over low heat until dissolved. Cool. In large bowl beat whipping cream and powdered sugar on high speed until stiff peaks form; fold gelatin into whipped cream. Place 1 cake layer on serving plate. Spread with 3/8-inch layer of whipped cream; top with half of cherries. Repeat; coat sides and top layer with remaining whipped cream. Pipe 8 rosettes around edge of cake; place reserved cherry on each. Scrape chocolate bar to form flakes. Press flakes on sides of cake; sprinkle on top. Store in refrigerator.

See Chef's Notes

SPA

Menus that are designed with an emphasis on lighter fare need not be reduced to plain and simple meals. Here, generous herbs and spices take the place of oils and cream sauces. The result, as one will attest, is a phenomenal goodness that defies conventional tastes.

NAUTICA
SPA

Poached Sole with Red Bean Ratatouille, p.142

141

POACHED SOLE WITH RED BEAN RATATOUILLE

SERVES 6

*W*hat a pure way to fully enjoy this delicate white fish. And the red bean ratatouille makes this dish complete.

½ cup	julienned leek
¼ cup	julienned onion
1	bay leaf
6	(8-oz. each) sole fillets
¼ cup	white wine
2 Tbsp.	lemon juice
¼ cup	chopped fresh dill
1 Tbsp.	corn oil margarine
Few	black peppercorns
1 Tbsp.	corn oil margarine
1 Tbsp.	chopped onion
½ tsp.	minced garlic
2 cups	cooked red beans
1 tsp.	chopped fresh thyme
1 tsp.	chopped fresh oregano
1½ cups	basic tomato sauce*
3 cups	diced zucchini

*I*n large frying pan place leek, onion and bay leaf; lay sole over vegetables. Pour wine and lemon juice over sole; add dill, margarine and peppercorns. Cook over high heat until mixture just comes to a simmer; reduce heat to low. Cover; cook until fish flakes with a fork.

Meanwhile melt margarine in medium saucepan over high heat; stir in onion and garlic. Cook until onion is tender. Stir in beans, thyme, oregano and tomato sauce. Reduce heat to medium; simmer 5 minutes to blend flavors. Add zucchini; cook 3 to 5 minutes or until zucchini is crisp-tender. Spoon onto individual serving plates. Place sole over red bean ratatouille.

*See Chef's Notes

GRILLED PORTABELLO MUSHROOM WITH ARUGULA SALAD

SERVES 6

*A*s portabello mushrooms become more accessible, an increasing number of people are tasting and believing what a wonderful food they can be. This will attract even more admirers.

HERB VINAIGRETTE

1 cup	olive oil
½ cup	balsamic vinegar
2 Tbsp.	chopped red onion
1 Tbsp.	chopped fresh basil
1 Tbsp.	chopped fresh thyme
1 Tbsp.	chopped fresh oregano
1 Tbsp.	minced garlic
1½ lb.	portabello mushrooms
½ cup	olive oil
6 to 8 cups	arugula greens
1	red bell pepper, chopped
2 oz.	garlic, cut into slivers, roasted

*I*n small jar with tight-fitting lid combine vinaigrette ingredients; shake well. Season to taste with salt and pepper. Set aside.

Remove stems from mushrooms. Wash stems and caps thoroughly. Slice stems into thick rounds. In large bowl toss mushrooms with olive oil. Place stems and caps on broiler pan. Broil 4 to 6 inches from heat 4 to 6 minutes or until mushrooms are tender, turning once. Cut mushroom caps into 4 or 6 triangles. Place caps and stems in baking pan; pour vinaigrette over. Cover; keep warm.

Divide arugula among 6 serving plates. Top with mushroom caps and stems. Garnish with red bell pepper and roasted garlic slivers. Drizzle with vinaigrette.

Tip: Mushroom caps and stems can also be cooked over hot coals on a charcoal grill.

Grilled Pacific Tilapia in Bok Choy with Grilled Oyster Mushrooms

Serves 4

*T*reat your guests to the ultimate in elegant dining. The suggested presentation is the quintessence of good taste.

Saffron and Cumin Tuile

10 Tbsp.	butter, softened
1	egg white
1 tsp.	vanilla
¼ tsp.	salt
¼ cup	all-purpose flour
½ tsp.	cumin
	Pinch saffron
¾ cup	tomato concasse*
¼ cup	chopped fresh rosemary
1 tsp.	olive oil
1 Tbsp.	olive oil
¼ cup	finely chopped onion
2 Tbsp.	finely chopped carrot
2 Tbsp.	finely chopped celery
¼ cup	béchamel sauce*
	Bok choy leaves, blanched
¾ cup	fish stock*
4	(4-oz. each) Pacific tilapia fillets
10	oyster mushrooms
	Rosemary sprigs
	Edible flowers
	Lemon butterflies

*H*eat oven to 375 degrees. In medium bowl beat butter until light. Gradually beat in egg white, vanilla and salt. In small bowl stir together flour, cumin and saffron. Beat slowly into butter mixture. Divide dough into 8 parts. On greased baking sheet place 4 rounds of dough. Dough will spread very thin when baking. Bake 6 to 8 minutes or until lightly browned. Working quickly with soft tuile carefully place over back of 6-oz. custard cups. Tuile will become crisp as it cools. Repeat forming 8 tuiles. Set aside.

In small bowl mix tomato concasse with rosemary; stir in olive oil. Set aside.

In small frying pan heat oil until hot over medium-high heat; stir in onion, carrot and celery. Cook until tender; remove from heat. Stir in béchamel sauce. Place blanched bok choy leaves in 8 (6-oz.) custard cups; divide vegetable mixture among cups. Bring leaves together to form balls. Heat fish stock in medium saucepan. Add bok choy balls; simmer 4 minutes.

Reduce oven to 350 degrees. Wrap tilapia in remaining bok choy leaves. Place on greased baking pan. Bake 18 to 20 minutes or until fish flakes with a fork. Arrange mushrooms around bok choy wrapped fish. Broil 4 to 6 inches from heat until mushrooms are tender. Bok choy should be lightly browned.

Place fish and mushrooms on serving plates. Place cooked bok choy balls in tuile; place on either side of fish. Pour tomato concasse at edge of fish. Garnish with rosemary sprigs, edible flowers and lemon butterflies, if desired.

See Chef's Notes

Tip: Bok choy wrapped tilapia may be grilled briefly over hot coals on a charcoal grill. Mark with crisscross pattern from grill while grilling. Reduce baking time to 15 minutes. Grill mushrooms, if desired.

MENU

VIVA L'ITALIA

Come celebrate the rich heritage of Italian dinning! Tonight, the beauty, charm, warmth and passion of every region flavor the chef's creations. Set aside all thoughts of the mundane as we salute the legacy of Caesar.

≈

INSALATA CALAMARI E MUSCOLI
SCAMPI PROVENÇALE

≈

MINESTRONE SOUP WITH PESTO
CREMA FUNGHI SOUP

≈

CAESAR SALAD

≈

SPAGHETTI CARBONARA
PENNE MARISCOS
VEAL PARMESAN
BREAST OF DUCK
WITH RASPBERRY COULIS

≈

TIRAMISÙ
CHERRIES JUBILEE

INSALATA CALAMARI E MUSCOLI

SERVES 6

Who says low-fat recipes have to be colorless and bland? This cold salad is bursting with flavor, and the combination of colors is positively picturesque.

DRESSING

2 Tbsp.	chopped onion
2 Tbsp.	chopped green bell pepper
2 Tbsp.	olive oil
1½ tsp.	lemon juice
¼ tsp.	minced garlic
¼ tsp.	chopped fresh thyme
	Hot pepper sauce
12 oz.	squid
1 Tbsp.	olive oil
12 oz.	cooked mussel meat, cut up
1½ cups	diced cooked potatoes
6	purple lettuce leaves
12	sliced radishes
6	lemon wedges
	Chopped parsley

In small bowl with tight-fitting lid combine dressing ingredients; shake well.

Brush squid with 1 Tbsp. olive oil; place on broiler pan. Broil 4 to 6 inches from heat until cooked. Cut into chunks. Mix squid, mussels and potatoes with dressing. Cover; refrigerate 6 to 8 hours.

Place lettuce on individual plates. Place about ⅓ cup salad on lettuce. Garnish with radish slices and lemon wedges; sprinkle with chopped parsley.

Steamed Whole Red Snapper in Tender Coconut Water and Lemon Grass

Serves 4

*H*ealthful entertaining can be accomplished with style and grace as demonstrated in this exquisite seafood plate. The baby vegetables are irresistible.

2	medium pears, peeled, cored
¼ cup	water
	Pinch saffron
¼ cup	fish stock*
4	whole headless red snappers
1 cup	sliced onion
¼ cup	chopped cilantro
1	stalk lemon grass, chopped
2 cups	tender coconut water
¼ cup	lemon juice
6 oz.	rice noodles
4	baby corn
4	baby yellow squash
16	fresh green beans
40	baby corn leaves
¼ cup	finely diced tomato
½ cup	low-sodium soy sauce
1 tsp.	cracked black pepper
	Toasted sesame seeds
4	lemon flowers
36	slices ripe olives

*P*lace pears and water in small saucepan. Cook over medium heat until tender; drain liquid. Add saffron and fish stock. Continue cooking, mashing pears, until thick puree is formed. Set aside.

Heat oven to 350 degrees. In roasting pan place snappers, onion, cilantro, lemon grass, coconut water and lemon juice. Bake 45 minutes or until fish flakes with a fork.

In medium bowl cover rice noodles with boiling water; let stand 15 minutes. Drain. Cook baby corn, baby squash and green beans until crisp-tender in small amount of water in small saucepan. Drain; keep warm.

Place 10 baby corn leaves on each plate. Roll rice noodles with fork into 4 nests and place over corn leaves. Add tomatoes to each. Place baby corn, baby squash and green beans on each plate. Remove fish from liquid; place on plates. Pour a little soy sauce over each. Top with pear coulis; sprinkle with black pepper and sesame seeds. Garnish with lemon flowers and ripe olives.

See Chef's Notes

TRILOGY OF SEAFOOD CARPACCIO WITH GREEN PEPPERCORNS, LEMON JUICE AND GARLIC CHIVES

SERVES 8

A trio of fresh, distinctive seafoods become center-of-the-plate main attractions. The crostini is loaded with taste and sorely missed without it.

DRESSING

¾ cup	lemon juice
¾ cup	olive oil
2 Tbsp.	minced garlic
½ tsp.	green peppercorns

CROSTINI

½ cup	chopped ripe olives
¼ cup	chopped onion
2 Tbsp.	garlic
4 tsp.	olive oil
½ cup	chopped green olives
16	thin slices French bread
½ cup	chopped tomatoes
12	(1½-oz. each) slices uncooked fresh swordfish
12	(1½-oz. each) slices uncooked fresh tuna
12	(1½-oz. each) slices uncooked fresh salmon
8 tsp.	green peppercorns
8 tsp.	chopped garlic chives

*I*n medium jar with tight-fitting lid combine dressing ingredients; shake well. Chill until serving.

In food processor bowl fitted with metal blade chop ripe olives; add 2 Tbsp. onion, 1 Tbsp. garlic and 2 tsp. olive oil. Process until paste is formed. Repeat using green olives. Spread ripe olive paste on 8 bread slices; top each with chopped tomatoes. Repeat with green olive paste. Place on broiler pan; broil until toasted.

On 8 serving plates pour about 2 Tbsp. dressing; arrange 1 slice of swordfish, tuna and salmon on each. Sprinkle each with 1 tsp. peppercorns and 1 tsp. chopped garlic chives. Garnish with chayote tops. Serve each with 2 crostini.

CHICKEN BREAST A LA GREQUE

SERVES 6

*C*hicken can be combined with such an infinite variety of marinades, herbs and vegetables that one never really has to have it the same way twice. This could very well be an exception.*

6	boneless skinless chicken breast halves
3 Tbsp.	olive oil
1 tsp.	chopped fresh thyme
1 tsp.	chopped fresh tarragon
1 tsp.	chopped fresh oregano
1 tsp.	minced garlic
½ tsp.	cracked black pepper
18	whole peeled shallots
4	artichoke bottoms, cooked, cut into 6 pieces each
18	black olives, cut in half
1 cup	chopped peeled tomato

*P*lace chicken in food storage bag. Add 1½ Tbsp. olive oil, ½ tsp. thyme, ½ tsp. tarragon, ½ tsp. oregano and ½ tsp. garlic to bag; seal bag. Toss to coat chicken with marinade. Marinate in refrigerator at least 30 minutes.

Remove chicken from marinade; place on broiler pan. Broil 4 to 6 inches from heat 10 to 14 minutes or until chicken is no longer pink in center, turning once.

Meanwhile, in small frying pan cook shallots in remaining 1½ Tbsp. olive oil until tender. Stir in remaining herbs, garlic, artichokes, olives and tomatoes; continue cooking until heated through. Season to taste with salt and pepper. Serve vegetables with chicken.

Tip: Marinated chicken can be grilled over medium coals on charcoal grill.

NAUTICA
SPA

Spa Pumpkin Pie

Serves 8

An extremely tasty pumpkin pie to be thankful for. It is low in calories, fat, sodium and cholesterol. Incredible.

Filling
1½ cups	cooked pumpkin
4 tsp.	NutraSweet®
1 Tbsp.	cornstarch
¾ tsp.	ginger
¼ tsp.	cinnamon
1⅔ cups	skim milk
½ cup	liquid cholesterol-free egg substitute
¾ tsp.	vanilla
1	(9-inch) frozen pie shell

Praline Sauce
½	recipe creme anglaise*
2½ Tbsp.	praline paste
8	strawberry fans

*H*eat oven to 350 degrees. In medium bowl combine all filling ingredients; whisk until smooth. Pour into pie shell. Bake 30 to 35 minutes or until center is set. Let cool on wire rack. Refrigerate until serving.

Remove 1 cup from warm creme anglaise; place in small bowl. Combine warm sauce with praline paste; mix until paste dissolves completely. Stir into remaining sauce. Chill.

Cut pie into 8 slices. Serve with 3 Tbsp. praline sauce and strawberry fan.

*See Chef's Notes

Tropical Fruit Medley

Serves 6

Sweet, luscious, unadorned fruit served the way it was meant to be. Simply refreshing.

1 cup	cantaloupe chunks
1 cup	watermelon chunks
1 cup	honeydew melon chunks
1 cup	fresh pineapple chunks
1 cup	red or green seedless grapes
6	Boston lettuce leaves
6	sprigs fresh mint

*I*n large bowl combine fruit; toss gently. Just before serving, line individual plates with lettuce; spoon fruit salad onto lettuce. Garnish with mint sprig.

SHRIMP AND LYCHEE IN LYCHEE PASSION FRUIT SAUCE

SERVES 8

*T*his lovely salad is a work of art. The shrimp cooked in sesame oil blends oh so nicely with the fruit.

10	lychees, peeled, pitted, chopped
	Juice of 6 passion fruits
2	mangoes
1 Tbsp.	sesame oil
24	uncooked medium shrimp, peeled, deveined
4 oz.	lollorosso lettuce or red leaf lettuce
1	head chicory, torn into bite-size pieces
24	lychees, peeled, pitted, quartered
	Chopped chives

*I*n small bowl combine chopped lychees and passion fruit juice; mix well. Chill until serving.

Peel mangoes; slice fruit lengthwise around large oval seed. Cut slices into 6 fans. In large nonstick frying pan heat sesame oil until hot over high heat. Add shrimp; cook until shrimp turn pink. Season to taste with salt and pepper. Divide lollorosso lettuce and chicory onto 6 salad plates. Place mango fans in center of each. Arrange 3 shrimp and 3 lychees around fans; pour lychee passion fruit sauce between shrimp and lychees. Sprinkle with chopped chives.

Tip: Shrimp may be cooked over hot coals on a charcoal grill. Brush with sesame oil.

STUFFED PEPPERS

SERVES 6

*W*hen eggplant, zucchini and peppers are at their peak, this is a "must try" entree that's bound to be a repeat everyone will love.

2 Tbsp.	olive oil
2½ cups	diced peeled eggplant
1 cup	chopped red bell pepper
1 cup	chopped red onion
1 cup	chopped mushrooms
1 cup	chopped zucchini
1 tsp.	minced garlic
1 tsp.	chopped fresh thyme
2 cups	cooked rice
½ cup	whipping cream
2 cups	basic tomato sauce*
6	whole green bell peppers, seeds and ribs removed, blanched

*H*eat oven to 350 degrees. In large nonstick frying pan heat oil over medium-high heat until hot. Add eggplant; cook, stirring occasionally until eggplant is soft. Mash eggplant. Stir in red pepper, red onion, mushrooms, zucchini, garlic and thyme. Cook 5 to 10 minutes or until vegetables are crisp-tender. Stir in rice and cream. Divide eggplant mixture among green peppers. Place in 13×9-inch baking pan; cover with tomato sauce. Bake 30 minutes or until heated through.

*See Chef's Notes

NAUTICA
SPA

CHEF'S NOTES

There is a cherished medley

of basic, required ingredients

that chefs simply whip up

without a thought. These

secrets are bound together

in this handy section that

can be referred to

again and again.

BASIC CHICKEN STOCK

YIELD 2 QUARTS

2 lb.	chicken bones
2 Tbsp.	margarine
2 cups	chopped onions
2 cups	chopped carrots
2 cups	chopped leeks
½ cup	chopped celery
12 cups	water
1 Tbsp.	black peppercorns
2	bay leaves
1	sprig fresh thyme

Place bones in saucepan; cover with water. Heat to a boil over high heat; simmer 5 minutes. Drain. In 4-quart stock pot melt margarine over medium-high heat; add onions, carrots, leeks and celery. Cook until softened; do not brown. Add water, peppercorns, bay leaves, thyme and chicken bones. Cook until mixture comes to a boil; reduce heat to low. Simmer 4 to 6 hours. Skim surface periodically.

Tip: The time the stock needs to be simmered depends on the strength of the stock desired.

BASIC CRÊPES

YIELD 20 CRÊPES

½ cup	all-purpose flour
½ tsp.	salt
1½ cups	milk
2 Tbsp.	butter, melted
3	eggs

In medium bowl whisk all ingredients together until smooth. Batter should be consistency of whipping cream. Refrigerate batter 30 minutes. Heat crêpe pan over medium-high heat until hot; brush with oil. Pour 3 Tbsp. batter into pan; tilt pan so batter covers bottom of pan. Cook crêpe until light brown on both sides, turning once. Repeat until batter is used. Cool crêpes. Place waxed paper between crêpes when stacking.

BASIC TOMATO SAUCE

YIELD 4 CUPS

2 Tbsp.	margarine
½ cup	chopped onion
¾ tsp.	minced garlic
4 cups	diced canned tomatoes
¼ cup	chopped fresh basil
¼ tsp.	dried oregano leaves
2	bay leaves
	Pinch of sugar

In medium saucepan melt margarine over medium-high heat. Stir in onion and garlic; cook until onion is tender. Stir in remaining ingredients. Reduce heat to low; simmer 20 minutes, stirring occasionally. Remove bay leaves.

BÉCHAMEL SAUCE

YIELD 4 CUPS

¾ cup	unsalted butter
1¼ cups	all-purpose flour
4 cups	milk
1	whole peeled onion
4	whole cloves
1	bay leaf

*I*n medium saucepan melt butter over medium heat; stir in flour. Cook 5 to 6 minutes; do not allow it to color. Remove from heat. In medium saucepan heat milk, onion, cloves and bay leaf over medium heat. When milk comes to a boil remove onion, cloves and bay leaf. Slowly add hot milk to butter-flour mixture, stirring constantly. Reduce heat to low; simmer 30 minutes. Strain; season to taste with salt and pepper.

BEEF STOCK

YIELD 4 CUPS

2 lb.	beef bones
1 cup	chopped onion
6 qt.	water
½ cup	chopped carrot
½ cup	chopped celery
4	bay leaves
1 Tbsp.	black peppercorns

*H*eat oven to 375 degrees. Place bones in roasting pan. Bake 1 hour or until bones are nicely browned. Add onions; continue roasting until onions are browned. Place water, carrot, celery, bay leaves and peppercorns in 8-quart stock pot; add bones and onion. Scrape any browned bits in roasting pan into stock pot. Bring to a boil over high heat; reduce heat to medium. Simmer 2 to 3 hours or until flavors are developed. Remove from heat; strain.

CAJUN SPICES

YIELD ABOUT ½ CUP

¼ cup	paprika
1 Tbsp.	salt
2 tsp.	pepper
2 tsp.	dried oregano leaves
2 tsp.	dried thyme leaves
2 tsp.	onion powder, if desired
2 tsp.	garlic powder, if desired
1 tsp.	cayenne pepper

*I*n small bowl combine all ingredients. Store in airtight container.

CHOCOLATE BUTTERCREAM

SERVES 5

½ cup	sugar
3½ Tbsp.	water
1 tsp.	light corn syrup
2	eggs
¼ tsp.	salt
1 cup	butter, softened
1 cup	semi-sweet chocolate chips, melted

*I*n small saucepan combine sugar, water and corn syrup. Bring mixture to a boil over high heat; boil 1½ minutes. In large mixer bowl beat eggs and salt on high speed until light. While beating on high speed, slowly pour hot syrup drop by drop into eggs. Continue to beat until mixture is light and fluffy and has cooled. Beat in butter on medium; continue beating 3 minutes. Add cooled melted chocolate; beat until light and fluffy, about 2 minutes.

Tip: Because of food safety, only pasteurized eggs should be used in recipes where the eggs are not cooked.

CHOCOLATE GANACHE

SERVES 5

9 oz.	semi-sweet chocolate, chopped
1 cup	hot whole milk
1½ tsp.	butter, softened

*P*lace chocolate in small bowl. Place bowl over simmering water; stir chocolate until melted. Pour in hot milk. Stir gently to mix; add butter. Remove from heat. Continue stirring until completely cooled and smooth.

Tip: Be careful that no water gets into chocolate or chocolate will seize.

CHOCOLATE PASTRY CREAM

SERVES 5 TO 6

5 Tbsp.	cornstarch
1½ cups	whole milk
2	egg yolks
¼ cup	sugar
3 Tbsp.	unsweetened cocoa
1 Tbsp.	unsalted butter

*I*n small bowl combine cornstarch, ½ cup milk and egg yolks; mix until well blended. Strain; set aside. In small saucepan combine remaining 1 cup milk, sugar, cocoa and butter; bring to a boil over medium heat. Boil 1½ minutes. Stir a small amount hot mixture into yolk mixture to warm. Gradually whisk warmed yolk mixture into hot milk mixture. Continue cooking, stirring constantly until mixture thickens and comes to a boil. Remove from heat. Place plastic wrap over surface to prevent skin from forming. Cool. Refrigerate if not using immediately.

CHOCOLATE SAUCE

SERVES 5

6 Tbsp.	sugar
¼ cup	unsweetened cocoa
2 Tbsp.	light corn syrup
½ cup	water
⅓ cup	semi-sweet chocolate chips, melted

*I*n small bowl combine sugar and cocoa; set aside. In small saucepan combine corn syrup and water; bring to a boil over medium heat. Boil 30 seconds. Add cocoa mixture; cook until sugar is dissolved, stirring constantly. Whisk melted chocolate into hot syrup. Remove from heat; stir gently until smooth. Sauce can be served hot or cold.

CHOCOLATE SPONGE CAKE

SERVES 5, 6-INCH CAKE

½ cup	sugar
4	eggs
¼ tsp.	vanilla
1¼ cups	sifted cake flour
2 Tbsp.	unsweetened cocoa

*H*eat oven to 375 degrees. Grease and flour 6-inch round cake pan. In medium bowl combine sugar, eggs and vanilla. Place over warm water; whisk constantly until mixture reaches 110 degrees. Sugar will be completely dissolved. Remove from water bath. Continue whisking until very light and fluffy. Sift flour and cocoa together; fold into beaten eggs. Pour into prepared pan. Bake 25 minutes or until cake springs back when touched lightly in center. Cool on wire rack. Cool completely before releasing from pan.

Tip: Purchase 6-inch round cake pan at specialty store with cake decorating supplies. If larger pan is used, baking time will decrease.

CREME ANGLAISE

SERVES 5 TO 6

6 Tbsp.	sugar
5	egg yolks
1 cup	whole milk
½ cup	whipping cream
1 tsp.	vanilla

*I*n top of double boiler mix sugar and egg yolks; whisk until light and lemon-colored. In small saucepan heat milk, cream and vanilla to scalding point. Remove from heat. Gradually add hot milk mixture to yolks, whisking constantly. Place over simmering water; cook, stirring constantly, until mixture coats the back of a spoon. Immediately remove from heat. Continue whisking until cooled, about 2 minutes. Sauce may be served hot or cold. If not used immediately store in refrigerator.

DEMI-GLACE

YIELD 4 CUPS

2 lb.	veal or beef shin bones
½ cup	chopped carrot
½ cup	chopped onion
½ cup	chopped leek
½ cup	chopped celery
3	cloves garlic, chopped
2 Tbsp.	tomato paste
16 cups	water
½ cup	red wine
½ tsp.	black peppercorns
1	bay leaf
½ cup	chopped tomato
3	sprigs fresh thyme

Heat oven to 425 degrees. Place bones in large roasting pan; roast 30 to 45 minutes or until lightly browned. Add vegetables and tomato paste. Roast 15 to 20 minutes, stirring occasionally. In 6-quart stock pot combine browned bones and vegetables with remaining ingredients; scrape any browned bits in roasting pan into stock pot. Bring to a boil over high heat; reduce heat to medium. Simmer 4 to 5 hours, skimming frequently. Broth should be reduced to about 4 cups. Remove from heat; strain through cheesecloth. Season to taste.

Tip: Broth can be thickened with ¼ cup roux (see Chef's Notes), if necessary.

DEVIL'S FOOD SPONGE CAKE

YIELD 1 CAKE, 8X8-INCH

1½ cups	sifted cake flour
5½ Tbsp.	unsweetened cocoa
3 tsp.	baking soda
½ tsp.	salt
¾ cup	sugar
½ cup	butter, softened
2	eggs
¾ cup	milk
1½ tsp.	light corn syrup
1 tsp.	vanilla

Heat oven to 350 degrees. Grease and flour 8×8-inch baking pan. In medium bowl sift together flour, cocoa, baking soda and salt; set aside. In medium bowl beat sugar and butter on medium until light and fluffy, about 3 minutes. Add eggs; beat until well blended. Stir in half of milk, the corn syrup and vanilla; beat until well blended. Fold in dry ingredients; mix well. Stir in remaining milk. Pour batter into prepared pan. Bake 30 minutes or until wooden pick inserted in center comes out dry. Cool on wire rack. When completely cooled remove from pan.

FISH STOCK

YIELD 4 CUPS

2 lb.	fish bones
3 qt.	water
½ cup	chopped onion
½ cup	chopped carrot
½ cup	chopped celery
1 Tbsp.	black peppercorns
4	bay leaves

Rinse fish bones in hot water. Place all ingredients in 4-qt. saucepan; bring to a boil over high heat. Skim surface. Reduce heat to medium; simmer 20 minutes. Strain.

Tip: Smoked salmon skin may be added while cooking to give broth a smoky flavor.

FONDANT

YIELD APPROX. 1 CUP

1 lb. powdered sugar
4 tsp. light corn syrup
1 egg white

*S*ift powdered sugar into medium bowl. Make a hole in center; add corn syrup and egg white. Mix until well blended. Knead mixture until smooth. Add a little water to thin. Place in top of double boiler; heat to 115 to 120 degrees before using.

Tip: Because of food safety only pasteurized eggs should be used in recipes where the eggs are not cooked.

GLACE DE POULET

YIELD 1 CUP

1 lb. chicken bones
3 qt. cold water
1 cup white wine
1½ cups chopped onions
1 cup chopped carrot
¼ cup chopped celery
¼ cup chopped leek
1 Tbsp. white peppercorns
1 bay leaf

*P*lace bones in 4-qt. stock pot; cover with water. Heat to a boil over high heat; simmer 5 minutes. Add remaining ingredients. Cook until mixture comes to a boil; reduce heat to low. Simmer 1 to 2 hours. Skim surface periodically. Strain. Return broth to stock pot. Bring to a boil over high heat; cook until reduced by three-fourths. Season to taste with salt and pepper.

HOT CHOCOLATE FUDGE SAUCE

SERVES 4 TO 5

¼ cup whipping cream
2½ Tbsp. butter
Pinch of salt
3½ Tbsp. unsweetened cocoa
2 Tbsp. sugar
2 Tbsp. brown sugar

*I*n medium saucepan heat cream, butter and salt to scalding point over medium heat. In small bowl mix cocoa, sugar and brown sugar. Whisk cocoa mixture into hot cream mixture. Continue cooking, stirring constantly, until sauce is thickened. Serve warm.

Tip: If sauce becomes too thick as it cools, reheat over simmering water.

ORANGE SAUCE

YIELD 2 CUPS

1½ cups	orange juice
2½ Tbsp.	cornstarch
½ tsp.	lemon juice
½ cup	sugar
2 Tbsp.	light corn syrup

*R*emove ¼ cup orange juice; mix in cornstarch and lemon juice. Set aside. In small saucepan combine remaining orange juice, sugar and light corn syrup. Bring to a boil over medium-high heat; reduce heat to medium. Boil 1 minute. Stir in cornstarch mixture. Continue cooking, stirring constantly, until thickened; cook 1 minute. Cool completely. Store sauce in refrigerator.

PINEAPPLE SAUCE

YIELD 1¾ CUPS

1	medium pineapple
1 Tbsp.	cornstarch
1 tsp.	pineapple extract
¼ tsp.	yellow food color
½ cup	sugar
2 Tbsp.	light corn syrup

*P*eel and core pineapple; finely chop pineapple. Remove ¼ cup; set aside. Place remaining pineapple in food processor fitted with metal blade; process until pureed. Strain puree; discard pulp. Remove ¼ cup strained puree; mix in cornstarch, extract and food color. Set aside. In small saucepan combine remaining puree, sugar and corn syrup. Bring to a boil over medium heat; stir in cornstarch mixture. Continue cooking, stirring constantly, until thickened; cook 1 minute. Stir in reserved chopped pineapple. Cool completely. Store sauce in refrigerator.

RED PEPPER COULIS

YIELD 4 CUPS

5	red bell peppers, seeds and ribs removed, cut-up
¼ cup	olive oil
1 Tbsp.	chopped shallots
½ cup	white wine
1 cup	chicken stock
½ tsp.	salt
¼ tsp.	pepper

*I*n large frying pan cook peppers in oil until tender over medium heat. Remove from oil; set aside. Stir shallots into remaining oil; cook until tender. Stir in white wine; scrape browned bits from pan. Stir in stock, salt and pepper; cook until reduced by half. In food processor fitted with metal blade puree peppers and shallot mixture. Season to taste.

Roasted Garlic Paste

YIELD ½ CUP

1 cup	garlic cloves, peeled
¼ cup	olive oil
½ tsp.	chopped fresh thyme
½ tsp.	chopped fresh oregano

*H*eat oven to 375 degrees. Place all ingredients in shallow roasting pan; add pepper to taste. Roast 20 to 30 minutes or until golden brown, stirring occasionally. Remove from oven; puree into fine paste. Season to taste with salt and pepper.

Roux

YIELD ABOUT 3 CUPS

1 cup	unsalted butter
1 cup	chopped carrot
1 cup	chopped celery
2	bay leaves
3¼ cups	all-purpose flour

*I*n medium frying pan melt butter over medium heat; stir in carrot, celery and bay leaves. Cook 1 minute. Stir in flour until well mixed. Reduce heat to low; cook 10 to 12 minutes or until flour is cooked but not colored. Stir occasionally. Cool completely. Remove bay leaves. Store in airtight container.

Tip: Prepare Brown Roux by cooking mixture until it is golden brown. Stir often so mixture does not burn.

Strawberry Sauce

YIELD 2 CUPS

2 cups	strawberries, finely chopped
2 Tbsp.	cornstarch
1 Tbsp.	pineapple extract
¼ tsp.	yellow food color
¾ cup	sugar
2 Tbsp.	light corn syrup

*R*emove ¼ cup chopped strawberries and set aside. Place remaining strawberries in food processor fitted with metal blade; process until pureed. Remove ¼ cup puree; mix in cornstarch, extract and food color. Set aside. In small saucepan combine remaining puree, sugar and light corn syrup. Bring to a boil over medium-high heat; reduce heat to medium. Boil 1 to 1½ minutes. Stir in cornstarch mixture. Continue cooking, stirring constantly, until thickened; cook 1 minute. Stir in reserved chopped strawberries. Cool completely. Store sauce in refrigerator.

TOMATO CONCASSE

YIELD 4 CUPS

4 lb.	ripe tomatoes
8 cups	water
½ cup	olive oil
1 cup	chopped onion
2 Tbsp.	minced garlic
½ tsp.	salt
¼ tsp.	white pepper
4	bay leaves

*I*n large saucepan bring water to a boil; add tomatoes. Cook 20 to 30 seconds. Remove tomatoes; plunge into ice water. Peel, seed and finely chop tomatoes. In large frying pan heat olive oil until hot over medium-high heat. Add onion and garlic; cook until onion is tender. Add salt, pepper, bay leaves and chopped tomatoes. Reduce heat to medium; simmer 3 to 5 minutes to blend flavors. Remove bay leaves.

VANILLA BUTTERCREAM

SERVES 5

½ cup	sugar
2	egg whites
1 cup	unsalted butter, softened
¼ tsp.	vanilla

*I*n small mixer bowl combine sugar and egg whites. Place over simmering water. Do not let water go higher than 120 degrees. Whisk whites until sugar is dissolved; remove from heat. Beat at high speed until stiff peaks form and mixture has cooled. Using medium speed gradually beat in butter and vanilla. Continue beating until mixture is smooth and fluffy.

Tip: Because of food safety, only pasteurized eggs should be used in recipes where the eggs are not cooked.

VANILLA CUSTARD SAUCE

SERVES 5

3 Tbsp.	cornstarch
1¾ cups	whole milk
2	egg yolks
1 tsp.	vanilla
¼ cup	sugar
1 Tbsp.	butter
½ cup	whipping cream

*I*n small bowl combine cornstarch, ½ cup milk and egg yolks; mix until well blended. Set aside. In small saucepan combine remaining 1¼ cups milk, vanilla, sugar and butter; bring to a boil over medium heat. Stir a small amount hot mixture into yolk mixture to warm. Gradually whisk warmed yolk mixture into hot milk mixture. Continue cooking, stirring constantly, until mixture comes to a boil. Remove from heat. Stir in whipping cream. Serve sauce warm.

Vanilla Pastry Cream

SERVES 5 TO 6

6 Tbsp.	cornstarch
1½ cups	whole milk
2	egg yolks
¼ cup	sugar
1 Tbsp.	unsalted butter
1 Tbsp.	vanilla

*I*n small bowl combine cornstarch, ½ cup milk and egg yolks; mix until well blended. Strain; set aside. In small saucepan combine remaining 1 cup milk, sugar, butter and vanilla; bring to a boil over medium heat. Stir a small amount hot mixture into yolk mixture to warm. Gradually whisk warmed yolk mixture into hot milk mixture. Continue cooking, stirring constantly, until mixture thickens and comes to a boil. Remove from heat. Place plastic wrap over surface to prevent skin from forming. Cool. Refrigerate if not using immediately.

Vanilla Sponge Cake

SERVES 5, 6-INCH CAKE

½ cup	sugar
4	eggs
¼ tsp.	vanilla
1¼ cups	sifted cake flour

*H*eat oven to 375 degrees. Grease and flour 6-inch round cake pan. In medium bowl combine sugar, eggs and vanilla. Place over warm water; whisk constantly until mixture reaches 110 degrees. Sugar will be completely dissolved. Remove from water bath. Continue whisking until very light and fluffy. Fold in sifted flour. Pour into prepared pan. Bake 25 minutes or until cake springs back when touched lightly in center. Cool on wire rack. Cool completely before releasing from pan.

Tip: Purchase 6-inch round cake pan at specialty store with cake decorating supplies. If larger pan is used, baking time will decrease.

Vegetable Stock

YIELD 4 CUPS

¼ cup	unsalted butter
½ cup	chopped shallots
1 cup	sliced carrot
1 cup	sliced celery
1 cup	sliced leek
¼ lb.	chicken bones, rinsed
6 cups	water
¾ cup	white wine
12	white peppercorns, cracked

*I*n 3-qt. saucepan melt butter over medium-high heat; stir in shallots. When shallots are tender, stir in carrot, celery, leeks and bones. Simmer 6 minutes. Stir in remaining ingredients; reduce heat to low. Simmer 30 minutes; strain.

INDEX

A

Ancho Honey Basted Atlantic Salmon, 94
Apple Pie, 106

B

Bahmi Goreng, 70
Baked Alaska, 134
Baked Mushroom Crêpes, 71
Baked Stuffed Apples, 116
Banana Cream Pie, 123
Banana Flambé, 115
Banana Pudding, 127
Basic Chicken Stock, 156
Basic Crêpes, 156
Basic Tomato Sauce, 156
Béchamel Sauce, 157
Beef Barley Soup, 28
Beef Stock, 157
Black Bean Soup, 39
Black Forest, 138
Blackened Pork Chops, 99
Blueberry Cobbler, 115
Blueberry State of Mind, 137
Bouillabaisse, 40
Braised Salmon with Roquefort and Celery, 97
Breast of Duck with Raspberry Coulis, 84
Broiled Beef - Bulgogi, 87

C

Caesar Salad, 30
Cajun Spices, 157
Cappuccino Pie, 102
Cheesecake, 138
Cherries Jubilee, 127
Chicken and Okra Soup, 43
Chicken Breast a la Greque, 149

Chicken Salad on French Baguette, 37
Chilled Cucumber Soup, 34
Chilled Key Lime Pie, 110
Chilled Shrimp Bisque, 40
Chilled Strawberry, 37
Chocolate Butter Cream, 158
Chocolate Cake, 116
Chocolate Decadence, 106
Chocolate Eclair, 120
Chocolate Fudge Cake, 124
Chocolate Ganache, 158
Chocolate Pastry Cream, 158
Chocolate Piece de Resistance, 119
Chocolate Sauce, 159
Chocolate Sponge Cake, 159
Chocolate Tres Leche, 128
Churrasco, 78
Cilantro Glazed Florida Snapper with Sesame Stir-Fry, 52
Coconut Cake, 130
Coconut Mousse Torte, 113
Coquilles Saint Jacques, 77
Cream of Asparagus Soup, 49
Cream of Broccoli Soup, 46
Crema Funghi, 44
Creme Anglaise, 159
Crêpes Suzette, 109

D

Darne de Salmon, 62
Demi-Glace, 160
Devil's Food Sponge Cake, 160

E

Escalope de Veau Calvados, 60
Escargot Bourgignonne, 10
Étouffée of Langoustine with Goat Cheese Zucchini Rosti, 33

F

Fillet of Fresh Alaskan Salmon, 56
Fish Stock, 160
Fondant, 161
French Crêpes, 13
Fresh Catch of the Day - Pan Fried with Rosemary & Roasted Garlic Beurre Noisette, 89
Fresh Garden Salad in a Walnut Vinaigrette with Sliced Pears, 24
Fried Calamari with Salsa Picante, 20
Fried Oysters, Remoulade, 15
Frog Legs with Rice Noodles, 12
Fruit Tranche, 105
Fruits de Mer, en Croute, 69

G

Gazpacho Andaluz, 34
Glace de Poulet, 161
Greek Salad, 43
Green Split Pea Soup with Smoked Sausage, 45
Grilled Jumbo Shrimp served over Mushroom Risotto, 55
Grilled New Zealand Lamb Chops, 77
Grilled Pacific Tilapia in Bok Choy with Grilled Oyster Mushrooms, 145
Grilled Portabello Mushroom with Arugula Salad, 142
Grilled Radicchio with Goat Cheese and Roasted Shallots, 16
Grilled Tenderloin of Pork with Sautéed Apple Slices, 73
Grilled Veal Chops Over Fine Herbs Galette with Cracked Coriander Port Wine Reduction, 88
Grilled Veal Chops with Herbs de Provence Sauce, 65
Guava Cream Cheese Napoleon, 124

H

Halibut Paupiettes with Lobster Stuffing, 63
Heat Cured Atlantic Salmon, 13
Hot Chocolate Fudge Sauce, 161
Hunan Filet of Beef, 96

I

Insalata Calamari e Muscoli, 146
Irish Cream Mousse Torte, 112

J

Jambalaya, 74
Jerk Cornish Hen, 93
Jumbo Shrimp Fra Diavolo, 84

K

Kahlua Cheesecake, 123

L

Lentil Soup, 36
"Lord Wellington" Baked Tenderloin of Beef, 87

M

Madras Vegetable Curry, 90
Mango Custard Tart, 134
Minestrone Soup with Pesto, 29
Mussels in Half Shell, 6

N

Napoleon, 120
Native Beans Salad, 46
Navy Bean Soup, 36
New Sirloin Steak "Martinique", 90

O

Oak Smoked Pork Loin with Champagne Cabbage, 81
Onion Soup with Cheese Croutons, 28
Orange Sauce, 162
Oriental Pekadilyo Soup, 44
Osso Bucco, 60

P

Paris Brest, 128
Passion Fruit Indulgence, 129
Pasta with Sun-Dried Tomatoes and Smoked Turkey, 78
Paupiettes of Salmon with Shrimp Mousse and Seaweed, 57
Penne Mariscos, 94
Penne Siciliana, 27
Penne with Vodka, Tomato and Caviar, 73
Pineapple Sauce, 162
Pizza Jardiniere, 19
Poached Pears, 137
Poached Sole with Red Bean Ratatouille, 142

Q

Quenelles of Fresh Alaskan Salmon, 59

R

Rack of Lamb, Natural, 52
Red Bean Soup, 39
Red Pepper Coulis, 162
Roasted Garlic Paste, 163
Roux, 163

S

Salmon Coulibiac, 66
Salmon Tortilla, 6
Satay of Chicken, 15
Sautéed Filet of Salmon in Pistazio Crust, 70
Sautéed Mushrooms, Champagne Sauce, 19
Scampi Provençale, 9
Seafood Newburg, 71
Shrimp & Lychee in Lychee Passion Fruit Sauce, 152
Shrimp Salad with Low Cal 1000 Island Dressing, 45
Smoked Salmon Parcels, 20
Sopa de Caracol, 49

Spa Pumpkin Pie, 151
Spaghetti Carbonara, 62
Steamed Whole Red Snapper in Tender Coconut Water and Lemon Grass, 148
Stir-Fried Prawns Hong Kong Style, 66
Strawberry Sauce, 163
Stuffed Chicken Leg with Langoustine Tail, 80
Stuffed Peppers, 152
Supreme de Poulet Farcie, 83
Swan Chantilly, 133

T

Tenderloin of Beef with Red Wine Mushroom Sauce, 69
Tequila Lime Shrimp, 12
Tiramisù, 102
Tomato Concasse, 164
Tomato Slices and Mozzarella Cheese, 27
Tournedos of Beef Tenderloin, 93
Trilogy of Seafood Carpaccio with Green Peppercorns, Lemon Juice & Garlic Chives, 149
Tropical Coconut Seafood, 89
Tropical Fruit Medley, 151
Trout Almondine, 83

V

Vanilla Butter Cream, 164
Vanilla Custard Sauce, 164
Vanilla Pastry Cream, 165
Vanilla Sponge Cake, 165
Veal Parmesan, 96
Vegetable Stock, 165

W

White Choco Bread Pudding, 130

Z

Zucchini and Eggplant Parmigiana, 99
Zucchini, Yellow Squash and Carrots Vinaigrette, 24

CARNIVAL CREATIONS